4WD

IN

1000

PHOTOS

CONTENTS

INTRODUCTION

The 4x4 has never been on such a high as these last few years – in fact it's been the only sector of the car market where sales have continually climbed. Yet things have only just begun. More and more manufacturers are entering the market, not least Volkswagen, Volvo and Porsche. A few years ago the very idea of a Porsche 4x4 would have seemed laughably improbable: now the Cayenne is selling so well that the doubters have had to eat humble pie.

Mostly the newcomers have veered more towards the SUV – or 'Sports Utility Vehicle' – end of the market, which begs the question of which niche will see the next bout of activity in this vibrant automotive sector. All the signs are that it will be in the 'soft roader' or 'crossover' class: vehicles such as the Lexus RX300 and the Mitsubishi Outlander point the way.

Faced with these challenges, the old guard are sure to react. The Land Rover company has already shown one path forward with its Range Stormer concept car, which prefigures a more sporting Range Rover. Will we also see a less overtly off-road contender from Jeep?

All this raises the issue of what will happen to those landmark reference vehicles, the Land Rover Defender and the Jeep Wrangler. To many people changing these classic designs would be a sacrilege. But you can't progress by standing still…

One thing is sure, it's going to be an interesting ride. So fasten your seatbelts, and let's take a look at the off-road world in all its fun and variety. Here's mud in your eye!

Serge Potier, who compiled this book.

A little bit of history

Building on the successful trans-Sahara expedition of two years previously, the Croisière Noire *of October 1924 to June 1925 followed a complex route, beginning in French North Africa and ending in Madagascar.*

The Croisière Noire *was divided into four expeditions. The first, led by Audouin-Dubreuil, headed for Mombassa; the second, led by Betembourg, had Dar es-Salaam as its destination; the third, with Haardt at its head, made for Mozambique; and finally Brull set off for the Cape. The story goes that nearly 40,000 natives cut a route through the equatorial jungle of the Belgian Congo for the expedition, because they believed it had been sent by 'Boula-Matari', otherwise known as famous British explorer Henry Morton Stanley.*

The Citroën *croisières*: tough, legendary and without parallel

1924–25, and after the success of the first crossing of the Sahara by car, with the 1922–23 Citroën half-track expedition, André Citroën took up a new challenge, the so-called *Croisière Noire*: this time the aim was to cross Africa from North to South. Georges-Marie Haardt and Louis Audouin-Dubreuil, the heroes of the Saharan venture, would lead the expedition. For greater efficiency, it would be split into four groups: the first would cross the Nile and the Rift Valley, the second would head for Dar es-Salaam, the third would set off for Mozambique, and the final group would cross Rhodesia and South Africa. After covering more than 3000 miles across Africa, fom Kampala to Livingstonia, via Nairobi and Mombassa, the expedition eventually reached the Cape. On 26 June 1925 all four groups met at Tananarive, on the island of Madagascar. Their total mileage was in the region of 17,000 miles.

One *croisière* can lead to another…and so in 1931–32 the *Croisière Jaune* took place, with the aim of linking the Mediterranean with the China Sea. Haardt and Audouin-Dubreuil led the 'Pamir' section, departing from Beirut, and another team, led by Victor

Point, left China. In all there were 40 people and 14 half-tracks following in the footsteps of Marco Polo.

Each group had to face a huge challenge: 'Pamir' had to cross the Himalayas, while Point's group, appropriately named 'Chine', had to cross the Gobi desert. In the mountains the intrepid explorers, always at risk of falling off a precipice, had to dismantle and rebuild their machines, so they could be carried in pieces across a section blocked by an avalanche. Then a tribal revolt in Afghanistan forced Haardt to change his route and enter Mongolia from India, across the high passes of the Himalayas.

After overcoming a thousand and one problems – not least with the articulated tracks constantly breaking – the two expeditions came together on 2 December 1931 and arrived in convoy in Peking on 12 February 1932, after having endured 7528 of the most demanding miles imaginable. But casting a shadow over this achievement was the death of Georges-Marie Haardt in Hong Kong on 16 March, from pneumonia. His memory lives on, fortunately, in the many books that recount the story of these extraordinary expeditions.

The crossing of the Wami river was harder than expected. Betembourg enrolled the locals, who were happy to lend a hand.

Although it might look as if the Citroëns have lost their tracks, this is an optical illusion: in fact they are towing specially-made trailers containing folding beds, mosquito nets, bedding material, shovels and pickaxes, and other essentials. In all the autochenilles, as they are called in French, covered over 17,000 miles across Africa.

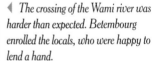

This famous poster is a reminder that the Croisière Noire, *a media event without parallel, excited massive interest in the scientific, artistic and economic worlds, with all the extraordinary stories that the expedition brought back. Some were more droll than others, such as how the Sultan of Maradi, the happy possessor of a 100-woman harem, agreed to allow it to be filmed on condition that the team repaired his car. Two mechanics took a look…and soon discovered the problem: the ignition hadn't been switched on!*

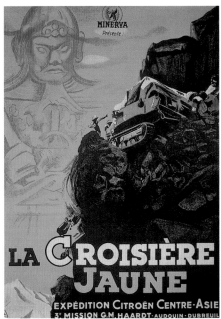

◀ The 'Pamir' group had to tackle the Himalayas – an extraordinary challenge. In one incident the track along a mountainside fell away under the weight of one of the Citroëns, and it took five hours with winches and slings to extricate the vehicle.

▶ The two teams were united on 2 December, and continued together to Peking, arriving in February 1932. The death of Georges-Marie Haardt from pneumonia cast a shadow over the end of the expedition.

LA CROISIÈRE JAUNE

EXPÉDITION CITROËN CENTRE-ASIE
3ᵉ MISSION G.M. HAARDT-AUDOUIN-DUBREUIL

◀ The Croisière Jaune was intended to link the Mediterranean with the China Sea, following in the footsteps of Marco Polo's Silk Route. Here Audouin-Dubreuil ponders the way forward…

▶ The vehicles used were half-track derivatives of the C4F and six-cylinder C6F Citroëns, specially equipped for the expeditions. The tracks were a constant weakness, so regular repairs were needed, as here.

▲ July 1931 saw the 'Pamir' group tackling the Bourzil pass in the Himalayas, at an altitude of 13,805ft. Clearly visible is the rotating drum to help surmount difficult obstacles. The vehicles were derived from the C4F and had a 30bhp engine.

▶ The six-cylinder half-tracks used by the 'Chine' group were visibly bigger; here one is tackling the Gobi desert, a prelude to the group being held prisoner for three months by a local warlord.

▲ Afghanistan in its splendour, with the famous Buddha carvings subsequently destroyed by the Taliban. But the 'Pamir' group was prevented from crossing the country by a tribal revolt, and had to divert 500 miles, via Kashmir.

▲ *In profile the Kégresse looks as solid as a house – this one weighs 2 tonnes. More importantly, it has a low centre of gravity.*

▲ *The disc front wheels seem almost fragile – but the secret of the half-track's abilities are in part down to the rotating front drum that helps deflect the vehicle from obstacles.*

▲ *The narrowness of the Kégresse was also a help, enabling it to be inched along narrow escarpements. The tracked rear was suspended on leaf springs and there was a transmission brake.*

Pioneer off-roader: the Citroën Kégresse

It looks like some sort of lash-up fit for nothing more than amateurishly crashing about the countryside. Yet the Citroën Kégresse has some adventures in its CV that fair numbers of 4x4s would envy. What's more, it's the most innovatory off-roader of all time, because before it came along there really wasn't much going on at all in this domain. The Kégresse pretty much set the ball rolling, being both the starting-point for a series of extraordinary expeditions and the vital tool that made these expeditions possible.

Its beginnings go back to 1913. A certain Adolphe Kégresse, inventor to his fingertips and the man in charge of Tsar Nicholas II's garage, decided to create a vehicle with sufficient off-road capability to cross marshes and cope with snowy terrain – useful attributes in the Russia of the time.

He accordingly came up with a car in which the drive at the rear was looked after by continuous rubber caterpillar tracks, with the undriven front end retaining normal tyred wheels. But Kégresse didn't have time to develop his ideas fully, as the Revolution broke out; so he returned to France, his country of birth, with his patents under his arm. He showed them to Jacques Hinstin, a long-time colleague of André Citroën, who in 1919 had begun production of his first car, the modest little Citroën Type A. Hinstin and Kégresse decided to manufacture four half-tracks and show them to André Citroën. The budding motor magnate fell under the spell and astutely decided to make the Kégresse – but also to use it as a way of garnering publicity, by using it for extravagant expeditions in the most far-flung parts of the world. André Citroën, as well as being a dynamic and trend-setting businessman, was in on the ground floor when it came to marketing!

◀ *The 30bhp engine of this example is a 1628cc sidevalve, devoid of fuel pump, with a gravity-fed horizontal carburettor.*
▶ *The manufacturer's identification plate on this Croisière Jaune type of half-track is situated in the middle of one of the track mechanism's swinging-arms.*

▲ *The front end of the Kégresse was always essentially that of the Citroën passenger-car of the time; sometimes the radiator shell was painted, sometimes it was plated.*

▼ The conventional front end uses a beam axle on semi-elliptic springs, with high-mounted friction dampers; the front wheels are braked.

▼ Just as with a tank, the tracks have a substantial operating length, thanks to the way the swinging-arms also act as tensioners. They are under their greatest strain when tackling really steep banks.

▼ The principal quality of the half-track is its extraordinary traction, thanks to those tracks: nothing stops it! The pay-off is a top speed which is no better than 25mph – if you're lucky, with a following wind!
▶ The tracks are also the Kégresse's Achilles Heel – a serious technical failing. Only three days into their expedition the vehicles that had left China on the Croisière Jaune had got through 14 tracks – their entire stock. André Citroën had to use the Trans-Siberian Railway to send a new consignment – consisting of 30 crates, each one 6ft long!

▲ The bench front seat offers nothing more than the most spartan home-comforts, while the dashboard contains only the bare essentials. Steering is heavy and has a poor lock – plenty of muscle is the basic requirement…

▲ The gearbox is a three-speed unit, unsynchronised, with a 'reverse H' pattern gearchange. The small lever alongside the gearlever and handbrake is to engage the reduction gearbox.

▲ This genteel little dip in the water would have made the teams on Citroën's expeditions smile, given what they had to go through when crossing the Sahara, Black Africa, or the far reaches of Asia.

▲▼ An electric starter is standard equipment, as on even the earliest Citroën cars, but sometimes the starting-handle has to be called into use.

▼ On board the Citroën-Kégresse you can't help living out all those pith-helmet fantasies…

▲ First of the line: one of the original Bantam pre-production models.

▲ The first Willys 'Quad': it was heavier than the Bantam but had a better engine. Note the different wing and frontal treatment.

▲ Ford's belated offering was the 'Pygmy'. Its performance in initial tests wasn't impressive, but its frontal styling was prophetic of the final Jeep style.
▼ The Willys MA was the chosen design: its body style was already evolving towards the recognised Jeep look we all know and love.

The first 4x4: the Willys Jeep

The Jeep was born of American army requirements for a lightweight all-terrain vehicle. By May/June 1940 a specification had been drawn up, and the design and manufacturing contract put out to tender. Included in the specification was four-wheel drive, a maximum speed on the road of not less than 50mph, and room for three soldiers and a machine-gun mounting. There were just two snags: the weight target was an unrealistic 11.6cwt, and after design approval the first vehicle had to be delivered within 39 days, followed by 70 further prototypes before a total of 75 days had elapsed.

Only two manufacturers responded, American Bantam and Willys-Overland, and it was Bantam that won the contract. By late September a prototype was ready, using Studebaker axles and a proprietary Hercules 1835cc sidevalve engine. Although having lost out in the initial bid, Willys-Overland went ahead with building its own vehicle: its design, called the Quad, was based on the Bantam, but it used the more powerful 2199cc Willys 'Go-Devil' engine.

The Willys was presented for testing in November…by which time Ford had entered the picture, having been approached by the Army, who felt they needed a large manufacturer on board. The result was two Ford prototypes based on the Bantam design and called the Pygmy.

There were now three different designs on offer, each very similar overall but differing substantially in detail, and in the end it was decided to award each firm a contract to build 1500 vehicles. This was a prelude to the commissioning body, the Quartermaster Corps, finally – in July 1941 – plumping for the Willys, and contracting Willys-Overland to build a first tranche of 16,000 Jeeps, known as the 'MA' type; the Toledo company was then engaged to build an 'MB' model, with an improved specification that shared as many components as possible with other US Army vehicles.

But as war demands increased, Ford was recruited at the end of 1941 to make the standardised Jeep, designated the GPW (for 'GP – Willys') alongside Willys. In the end wartime production of the GPW was 361,349 by Willys and 277,896 by Ford.

▶ Franklin D Roosevelt aboard a Willys Jeep. Paradoxically, the US Lend-Lease policy meant that the USSR was among the first to profit from the Jeep.

▶ *Echoing a cavalryman faced with the sad necessity of shooting his dying horse, this drawing evokes the affection felt for their Jeeps by US servicemen in the Second World War.*

Copyright 1944 by Bill Mauldin

▼ *This is the first attempt at a French Jeep, a prototype for what became the over-complex and unsuccessful Delahaye VLR.*

▲ *The Jeep came to the notice of the French during the D-Day landings in Normandy. Churchill said that the Jeep helped win the war.*

▼ *After the failure of the VLR, the decision was taken to have Hotchkiss manufacture the MB Jeep under licence.*

561 BHG 91

▲ *Recognisable by its bigger headlamps, this is the first Jeep for the general public, the CJ-2A of 1946. 'CJ' stands for 'Civilian Jeep'.*

▲ *After the war, the MB Jeep was soon put to work, not least in agriculture.*

▲ *Here it is all kitted out as a fire-brigade rapid-response vehicle…*

▲ *….and here is a later civilian Jeep as a smart little breakdown truck.*

▲ *The Jeepster of the 1948–50 model years was not a success; four-cylinder and six-cylinder models were available.*

▶ *The Jeep still exerts a powerful emotional pull for Americans, as this 1980s publicity photo shows so clearly.*

The Jeep: evolution of the marque, from 1941 to today

▲ *The MB Jeep, follow-up to the MA pre-series, was produced for many years and can be found on all corners of the planet.*

▲ *After the MB, Willys launched a civilian version called the CJ2 ('CJ' standing for 'Civilian Jeep'), from which in turn evolved the M38 military Jeep.*

▼ *The M38 A1 Jeep is more than just a development of the M38: it is bigger, partly because of its more powerful 71bhp Hurricane 2.2-litre engine, and anticipates the Jeep of today in its basic styling.*

▼ *The M38 having become too big, not least as an air-portable, there was a need for a smaller Jeep. Consequently in 1959 Ford came up with the M151 'Mutt', with its all-independent suspension. It was still being used by the US Army up until the end of the 1980s.*

The Jeep has always stayed a simple, basic, popular vehicle. However, on various occasions, right from the outset, there have been initiatives to broaden the range, and lessen dependency on the core model, the MB Jeep and its successors. There have been a few flops and a few missed opportunities, but finally Jeep has emerged as one of the premier 4x4 brands in the world. This has been very much to the benefit of the US Chrysler group, which has owned Jeep since 1987 – and which has itself been part of the German Daimler concern since 1998.

But there was an earlier European connection, when Renault was in alliance with previous proprietor American Motors, in which it ultimately became a majority shareholder, and the Jeep was distributed in Europe by the French marque; as a consequence it was possible to buy a Jeep CJ7 with a petrol or diesel Renault engine, while the Cherokee was offered – and sold well – with the 2.1-litre turbo-diesel more unusually found under the bonnet of the Renault 21.

Our picture-spread traces the evolution of the Jeep over six decades and three principal model families, a progression that has always managed to keep alive the spirit of that first Willys MB, right through to the latest versions of the Wrangler, a vehicle that excites as many passions as its military forefather.

▼ *The civilian version of the M38 A1 is universally known as the 'CJ'; this is a CJ5, as first seen in 1955. It was available with sundry different power units – four-cylinders (2.2-litre and 2.4-litre), in-line 'sixes' (3.8-litre and 4.2-litre), an ex-Buick V6, and even a 120bhp V8.*

▲ *The CJ7 was the first civilian Jeep to be widely available in Europe – not least in France, where it was imported by Renault from 1978. It was technically much as the CJ5, whose engines it inherited. Three versions were offered: Standard, Renegade and the luxury Laredo.*

▲ *The CJ6 was a long-wheelbase Jeep intended for the utility market, and was rarely exported to Europe.*

▲ *The TJ series has only changed in detail since its launch, but there have been countless limited editions, such as this 'Twin Spirit' model.*

▲ *In summer 1983 the 3-door and 5-door Cherokee arrived; they were smaller than their predecessors.*

▲ *The Jeep Wrangler appeared in September 1986. It broke with styling tradition in having rectangular headlamps, and was powered by either a 2.5-litre 'four' or a 4-litre in-line 'six'.*

▲ *The TJ of 1996 brought back round headlamps, and now had all-round coil-spring suspension instead of a beam axle. The engines kept the same capacity as before but were new units.*
▼ *The 1998-introduced Grand Cherokee (right) with the preceding version of 1992 and (left) the Grand Wagoneer, of which production ended in 1991. The Grand Wagoneer label had been introduced with the arrival in 1983 of the first Cherokee.*

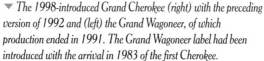

▲ *September 2001 saw the launch of the new Cherokee, which benefited from more internal space, independent front suspension and a new range of engines, as well as softer lines.*
▼ *The Grand Cherokee has entered its third generation for 2005, and now has independent front suspension. There is also rack-and-pinion steering and a new five-link coil-sprung rear axle; petrol engines are V6 and V8, with a range-topping 5.7-litre 'Hemi' V8.*

◄ *In 1946 Willys introduced an all-steel Jeep station wagon and for 1948 this was joined by the Jeepster, a supposedly sporting four-seater open tourer created by freelance stylist Brooks Stevens. Sometimes referred to as the Phaeton, the Jeepster was not a success and was withdrawn in 1950.*

The Land Rover saga

▲ The first prototype of 1947 had a central steering wheel and used a Jeep chassis; the engine was the ohv 1389cc Rover Ten unit, but production cars used the 1595cc IoE Rover 60 'four'.

▲ The Land-Rover soon became popular in 'colonial' roles. The headlamps emerged from behind the grille in May 1950.

level. Aluminium, however, was in reasonable supply.

Thinking back to that Jeep on the Wilks farm, an idea crystallised: while waiting for steel to come off-ration, Rover could make an aluminium-bodied multi-purpose Jeep-like utility vehicle. The car would merely be a stop-gap, made with the least possible investment in presses and tooling. It could have a simple Jeep-inspired ladder frame, and a rudimentary body made largely of straightforwardly-folded aluminium. Using existing Rover car mechanicals, the vehicle could be introduced in relatively short order, and should find a ready market with farmers seeking a working vehicle that could at the same time be used off the farm; with sundry power take-offs it could combine the functions of both tractor and family car.

The first prototype, built on a Jeep chassis and having a central steering wheel, was finished in mid-1947 and the first 25 cars left the lines at Rover's Solihull works at the end of the year. Formal production was underway by the summer of 1948. Today's Defender is still related to those first vehicles, and the Land-Rover has gone on to be one of the best-loved 4x4s in the world, famed for its ruggedness, its mechanical simplicity, and for its rust-resistant aluminium bodywork, which remains a key feature. Not bad going for a stop-gap born of the desperation of early post-war Britain!

Rover chief engineer Maurice Wilks was a gentleman-farmer in his spare time, with a farm on the island of Anglesey. For general farm duties just after the war he used a de-mobbed Willys Jeep, but the question of what would replace this faithful workhorse when it finally pegged out was a difficult one: another ex-Army Jeep, he supposed.

Meanwhile the Rover company was struggling, in a post-war Britain where the government only allocated rations of steel to motor manufacturers on the basis of export performance. Rover had no tradition of exporting, so risked not getting sufficient steel to relaunch car production at a satisfactory

▲ This early Series I still has the 1595cc engine: from August 1951 this was replaced by a larger 1997cc unit. In the first full year 8000 Land-Rovers were made, but by the second year output was more than 16,000 cars.

▲ The first long-chassis models arrived in autumn 1953, on a 107in wheelbase. This is the station wagon; other styles were a pick-up (with canvas or metal top) and a pick-up with a full-length hardtop.
◀ This was not the first station wagon: in 1948 an ash-framed estate had been announced, on the original 80in wheelbase. Bodied first by Abbey Panels and latterly by Mulliners of Birmingham, it was not a success and was deleted in 1951.

▲ *This Series II lwb station wagon – recognise it as an SII by its sill 'skirts' – has the 109in wheelbase introduced in 1956; the Series II was launched in 1958.*

▲ *The Range Rover was introduced in June 1970: powered by the ex-Buick 3.5-litre V8, it retained a separate ladder chassis but had coil-spring suspension.*

▲ *In 1971 the SIII Land Rover replaced the SIIA introduced in 1962; it is recognisable by its plastic grille. Headlamps had moved to the wings in 1968–69.*

▲ *The 88in 'Lightweight' built for the British army entered service in 1968, and was intended for air-portable duties.*

▼ *It was only in 1981 that a four-door Range Rover arrived – roughly nine years after the first prototype had been built. Automatic transmission became available for 1983.*

▲ *Underneath their largely unchanged bodywork, the '90' and '110' models launched in 1983 used Range Rover coil-spring suspension and had permanent 4wd. Subsequently they adopted the 'Defender' name.*

▲ *The Discovery was in essence a cheaper version of the Range Rover, and was launched in 1989 –at first only as a three-door. Power units were initially either the V8 or a 2.5-litre turbocharged direct-injection diesel.*

▲ *The Range Rover was replaced by an all-new model in 1994, powered either by a 4.0-litre or 4.6-litre V8 or a BMW 2.5-litre turbo-diesel straight-six.*

▲▼ *In 1998 the Land Rover celebrated its 40th birthday. It was now a marque in its own right, and the Freelander had just joined the range as a fourth line, available as a three-door and a five-door.*

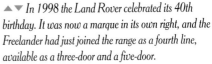

▲ *With the disposal of Rover by BMW in 2000, Ford took over Land Rover – and inherited the third-generation Range Rover subsequently launched in 2002.*

▼ *The second-generation Discovery, meanwhile, was facelifted in June 2002, gaining new front and rear lights and revised brakes and suspension.*

▲ *The first of the line, the '80in', has simple lines in largely flat aluminium. Just as with the Willys Jeep that inspired it, the windscreen folds flat.*

▲ *The wheels stuck out firmly at each corner help the Land-Rover's off-road ability by giving excellent angles of attack.*

▲ *The earliest type of seats have curved rather than squared-off backrests.*

▲ *From the start there was a two-range transfer box, and a freewheel, as on Rover cars, was used until 1950 – at which stage 4wd became selectable in high-range rather than permanently engaged.*

▼ *The rear has featured a drop-down tailgate from the start; exterior door handles only came in during 1952.*

▼ *Only the latest Td5 Defender is needed to complete Philippe de Rochefort's superb private collection.*

The Land Rover through the ages: 1948–70

The Land Rover name is really all about one model, today called the Defender, and which all things considered has barely evolved much in either its mechanicals or its look. That's because it has always had an extraordinary rightness about its design. Thus today's Defender still has an aluminium body, is still largely rustic in its conception, and still has the same unchallengable off-road capabilities as it had at its launch in 1948.

Time has not wearied it, and you can be sure that most owners would be happy for its basic concept to remain unchanged in the years to come. Perhaps the best guarantee of this is the 4x4 fad itself, which has helped protect and promote the Land Rover, on the basis of its remarkable off-road performance as much as anything.

With Ford having acquired Land Rover from BMW in 2000, the company is seeing generous investment in new models and in new production facilities. Inevitably this will result sooner or later in a new Defender. Fortunately the men at the top seem to have an astute understanding of the marque's traditions and values.

The Defender of the future will certainly have a tough no-nonsense look, making reference to the model's illustrious past, but will still be every inch a Defender. That much is vital: it is, and will remain, the cornerstone of the marque's identity, and it must continue to be worthy of its lineage.

Here, in two spreads, you can see how the Land Rover has evolved over six decades, from the little '80in' of 1948 to the Td5 Defender of today.

◀ *The original 1595cc engine, developing 50bhp, was replaced by the 2-litre unit in 1951; at 52bhp it was barely more powerful, but torque rose from 80lb ft at 2000rpm to 101lb ft at 1500rpm.*

▲ Supplementary cooling apertures appeared behind the grille on the SII, an indication that it had a more powerful engine.
▼ This was indeed the case, with a new 2286cc ohv engine replacing the old IoE unit; it was derived from the 2052cc diesel introduced in June 1957.

▲ The Series II retained the 88in and 109in wheelbases introduced in 1956, but there was an extra 1½in of width, which gave a wider track and better stability; the body sides had more form, too.

▲ A revised dashboard with two matching larger-diameter dials was introduced in 1953 with the arrival of the 86in and 107in models and was carried over largely unchanged to the Series II.

◀ Recessed exterior door handles had been introduced on the Land Rover in 1954.

▲ The angular lines of the 'Lightweight' were a function of its simplified and lighter panelling.

▲ The Army 'Lightweight' was made from 1967 until 1985; with the doors, screen, tailgate, spare wheel and weather equipment removed, it weighed 23.75cwt, a saving of nearly 3cwt over a regular SIIA.

▲ The yellow-knobbed lever selects four-wheel drive and the red-topped lever low or high range.

▲▶ White-on-black instruments transcended fickle fashions; take the 90mph maximum reading with a pinch of salt!

▲ The 'Lightweight' generally used the 2.3-litre petrol 'four', but some had the diesel engine.

▲ *This long-wheelbase '109' SIII has the standard canvas tilt; windows are still sliding, as they are on the first 90/110 models.*

▲ *The headlamps moved to the wings on later SIIA models; the grille would normally be silver rather than black.*

▲ *This swb Defender has a version of the styled steel wheels used on the original Range Rover.*

▲ *On the Series III the instruments moved to in front of the driver; trim was as spartan as ever.*
▼ *The 2286cc petrol and diesel 'fours' gained a five-bearing crankshaft in 1981 and were carried over to the 90/110 range.*

The Land Rover through the ages: from 1971 to date

The Series III announced in September 1971 was an interim model, with more robust mechanicals, but keeping the same engines as before and still using leaf-spring suspension fore-and-aft. An appreciated improvement, all the same, was a new gearbox with a synchronised bottom gear. Less appreciated was the new plastic grille, which was lamentably unsuited to being unscrewed and used as a barbecue griddle, unlike the wire item it replaced. From 1979 a V8 version of the '109' was available, with a detuned 91bhp version of the all-aluminium Rover-Buick V8; this replaced the in-line 'six' available as an option on the 109in model since 1967.

Plans were afoot for an all-new Land Rover for the 1980s, but in the end funds did not allow this, and so the SIII was upgraded with a new chassis to make the '90' and '110' of 1983; the body stayed the same, but for a new flat front with a grille set level with the wings, a one-piece screen, and the fitment of plastic wheelarch extensions to cover the new model's wider track. Gradually refined over the years, these coil-sprung models are today known as the Defender, and with the 2004 demise of the V8 the sole engine fitted is the Td5 2.5-litre direct-injection five-cylinder.

▲ ▶ *The zebra-painted look here recalls the Daktari TV series.*

▲ *The forward-positioned radiator grille, first seen in a different form on the V8-powered '109', identifies the 90/110 series.*

▲ *The dashboard was marginally more car-like; there was now permanent 4wd, with a diff lock.*

▲ *Various power units have been used over the years, including the petrol V8 in this example, where it is fuelled by twin SU carbs.*

▲ *The Defender as it is today, powered by the Td5 turbo-diesel; this is a swb station wagon.*

▲ *A driver's airbag is standard, but otherwise the cockpit is largely unchanged.*
▼ *The five-cylinder diesel engine deveops 122bhp and 221lb ft of torque at 1950rpm.*

▲ *The 'Defender' badge and the oval 'Land Rover' badge are giveaways that this is a later version of the 90/110 series.*

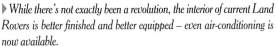

▲ *The Defender 300 Tdi benefits from a highly-regarded and modern new direct-injection engine. Still a 2.5-litre four-cylinder unit, its power has risen from 107bhp to 113bhp.*
▷ *While there's not exactly been a revolution, the interior of current Land Rovers is better finished and better equipped – even air-conditioning is now available.*

▲ *The turbo-diesel engine is more powerful and offers better refinement than earlier units.*

▲ *This photo shows the three wheelbases offered; a 90in hardtop, a 110in station wagon, and a 130in double-cab pick-up.*

The Land Rover in its many guises

▲ *This 1966 Series IIA was used by Queen Elizabeth II as a military parade vehicle for inspecting the troops.*

▲ *This Series I long-wheelbase ambulance was used on Guernsey; the body is unusually tall.*

The Land Rover was originally available only as a tiny 80in-wheelbase open pick-up; in 1954 the wheelbase went up to 86in and the long-chassis '107' was introduced. Two extra inches were put into the wheelbase of both variants in 1956, to create the '88' and the '109'. What all this meant was that with the choice – from June 1957 – of a petrol or a diesel engine, there were endless permutations of Land Rover possible.

But that wasn't enough for a buying public that had been seduced by the Land Rover's ruggedness and versatility. As a consequence specialist creations such as ambulances, fire-tenders, royal parade cars and even tracked Land Rovers have been built over the years, with Land Rover setting up its own Special Projects Department to develop out-of-the-ordinary adaptations of the standard vehicle.

These oddballs have a unique appeal, and make a big Land Rover gathering a wonderful experience for those who have never before seen a six-wheeled Land Rover or any of the bizarre military versions produced over the years. Dial in the forward-control models, both civilian and military, and the various licence-built foreign Land Rovers, such as those made in Spain by Santana, in Germany by Tempo and in Belgium by Minerva, and you have the richest of 4wd cocktails. This selection of photos only scratches the surface…

▲ *The Land Rover was popular as an airfield fire-tender, as this fully-equipped SIII testifies.*

▲ *Originally painted in pink for desert use, so it could blend in with the pink desert haze, this military version of the Land-Rover was one of the famous 'Pink Panthers'.*

▲ *The sloping front of this Land Rover marks it out as a Belgian-built Minerva of the 1950s.*

▲ *The Series I 80in station wagon was short-lived; this is a rare survivor.*
◀ *This Series I was a rapid-intervention vehicle for a local fire brigade.*

▲ *Both civilian and military forward-control Land Rovers were made over the years; this would appear to be an adaptation of a V8-powered military '101' model.*

▲▼ *Never mind their age, old Landies can still cut it in the toughest off-road competitions.*

▲ *The 88in 'Lightweight' is a popular choice for 'green-laning'.*

▲ *The '109' in its element: jerrycans and sand-mats mean it's equipped for the worst.*

▼ *A high driving position and slab sides help position the Land Rover.*

▲ *Extended-chassis version of the twin-cab '130': all six wheels are driven!*

▼ *Flower-power Land Rover '109': very hippy-dippy…*

▲ *For an off-the-beaten-track camper van you can't beat a kitted-out '109'.*

▲ *Mmm! Nice! A restored Series I short-wheelbase model; ripply panels are quite authentic…*

Toyota's workhorse: the Land Cruiser

▲ *The first Toyota 4x4 appeared in 1951. It looked remarkably like the original Willys Quad prototype of 1940.*

▲ *A six-cylinder engine was always in the picture.*

▲ *Still not ready to enter production, the lines of the BJ25 were clearly Jeep-inspired.*

▲ *Later cars had an identifiable Land Cruiser snub nose – and the Land Cruiser name.*

Japan, 1929. Sakichi Toyoda, a Japanese industrialist and the inventor of an automatic cotton loom, had decided to pass to his son Kiichiro the profits from the sale of manufacturing rights to the English. A lover of cars, Toyoda's eldest son launched into the design and manufacture of engines. Soon Toyoda became Toyota, which was easier to pronounce and more to the point incorporated the seven Japanese symbols for prosperity and success.

In 1938 a total of 10,000 vehicles left the lines of the Toyota Motor Corporation. But in 1945, after the capitulation of the Imperial army, the Japanese motor industry fell into the hands of the Americans. In 1947, a key date in Japan's reconstruction, TMC launched the B85, a right-hand-drive replica of the MB Jeep. During the 1950s a series of prototypes were developed, carrying the BJ name. Then the company engineers decided to climb Mount Fuji in a pair of BJs.

They failed, a few feet from the summit, but managed to get higher up the mountain than any other vehicle had succeeded in doing. The achievement was sufficiently remarkable to impress the police, who duly adopted the BJ.

Still clearly Jeep-derived, but with germs of the trademark Land Cruiser front, the Toyota 4x4 was launched in 1953 as the BJ25, taking the Land Cruiser name in 1954. In fact, if we're strictly accurate, only the four-cylinder diesel was coded 'BJ': the six-cylinder petrol-engined Land Cruiser was known as the 'FJ' and the six-pot diesel as the 'HJ'.

But the 'BJ' tag became common currency for the range, which became popular in all corners of the world. In 1965 the 50,000th Land Cruiser left the lines; in 1981 the millionth was made, and the Toyota became one of the best-selling 4x4s in the world. For some fans there's only one Toyota off-roader, and that's the Land Cruiser.

▶ *In 1958 Toyota launched the FJ25 Land Cruiser, one of the most powerful off-roaders in the world. The engine was a 3.9-litre petrol 'six' developing 105bhp, an extraordinary output for the time.*

▼ *Success was immediate. The canvas doors have given way to steel items with wind-up windows and there are springs derived from those of the Toyota Crown car, rather than unyielding ex-lorry springs.*

▼ *The body underwent several evolutions during the decade: this magnificent FJ35 station wagon echoed Jeep's own all-steel wagon.*

◀ *In 1953 the BJ was beginning to gain an identity of its own, with this BJ25.*

▼ By 1958 the principle of two different wheelbases had been established, with the FJ28 having an extra 6in between the wheels compared to the FJ25.

▼ Goodbye FJ25, FJ28 and FJ35; hello FJ40, FJ43 and FJ45. From 1962 the Land Cruiser had a new identity and a new look that would last for more than 20 years.

▲ At that time the F-type engine developed 125bhp, thanks to a raised compression ratio. A new transfer box and new reduction gearing meant off-road ability took a giant step forward.

▲ Here is a splendid example of the mid-sized FJ43 of the 1960s, a decade which saw the Land Cruiser achieve commercial success, racking up its 100,000th sale in 1968.

▼ This HJ45 had a long chassis and a six-cylinder in-line diesel of 3.6 litres, developing 86bhp. The Toyota name was now spelt out on the grille.

▶ In response to the 1973 fuel crisis Toyota relaunched the four-cylinder B-series, with an economical 76bhp 3-litre engine, as the BJ40 and BJ43.

▲▼ By the time of the BJ41 and BJ44, the replacements for the BJ40 and BJ43, the windscreen wipers had migrated to the bottom of the screen and there were disc front brakes, a floor-mounted handbrake and a 19-gallon petrol tank. Bodies available included canvas-top and hardtop styles, with a pick-up available on the long wheelbase. The FJ had also evolved, with 135bhp thanks to an enlarged 4.2-litre engine.

◀▼ The final evolutions of the 40-series cars were the BJ42 and the middle-wheelbase BJ44, both using the new 3B engine. This developed 90bhp, with maximum torque of 159lb ft at 2200rpm. With front discs, a five-speed gearbox and power steering, this was a dream come true!

▲ In 1984 a page was turned: the BJ70 series replaced the venerable 40-series. Efficiency took a leap forward, but the retro look had gone. For true fans the 'BJ' name means only one thing: the BJ40 series.

▲ *This first prototype of 1948 was unsurprisingly similar to a Jeep – although its weather protection was clearly superior. Under the bonnet, even at this early stage, there was a six-cylinder engine.*

◀ *It was with the 60-series (here a swb G6) that the Patrol became a serious player in the 4wd market.*

▲ *This is the first vehicle to carry the Patrol name – the 4W60 model of 1951 – and the front styling has already evolved. The long-stroke 3670cc 'six', mated to a three-speed gearbox, gave impressive low-range torque.*

▲ *Three years later, and the G4W65 Station Wagon had appeared, bearing the Carrier name. The engine now pushed out 92bhp, or 105bhp in later cars.*

Nissan Patrol:
the Japanese Land Rover?

Just like Land Rover, the engineers at Nissan quickly understood, after the Second World War, the value of having a Jeep-like vehicle in their range. At the end of the 1940s Japanese industry, and especially the car industry, was pretty much on its knees. A lightweight 4wd had a very real appeal: the road network was in a miserable state and the national economy not much better, two factors that made a rugged low-cost vehicle seem an attractive proposition. At the same time the government and the army were keen to have the motor industry build a rapid-intervention vehicle along the lines of the Jeep – something useful to the military but also practical civilian transport from which pick-up and van versions could be spun off.

The result, in 1951, was the first Nissan 4x4, made possible by a commercial agreement with the US which opened the perspective of an export market for the vehicles. From the start the name Patrol was used, attached to a car that like so many 4x4s of the time was closely related to a Jeep in its utilitarian looks.

Where it stood apart was in its engine: signalled by a longer bonnet than that of a Jeep, it was an in-line six-cylinder unit of 3670cc, developing 85bhp at 3600rpm and an impressive 173lbs ft of torque at 1600rpm. When a Jeep was only pushing out 60bhp, and 106lbs ft of torque at 2000rpm, that was quite a bit of extra muscle. Putting this proven engine, which came from the NT85 lorry, in the lighter 29.5cwt Patrol resulted in an unstressed performance that helped establish Nissan's legendary reputation for reliability. Since then, the six-pot has been a characteristic feature, although now it has been joined by a new 16-valve 'big four'.

▲▶ *The next evolution of the Patrol is represented by this 60-series of 1960 with its overhead-valve engine developing 125bhp at 3400rpm and a hefty 210lb ft of torque. The gearbox is an all-synchro four-speeder and alongside the gearlever are the levers for the high-low transfer box and for engaging or disengaging 4wd.*

▲ *From this angle the 60-series has something of the Toyota BJ about it. It could be kitted out with a mechanical winch at the front, while at the rear there was still a power take-off. This type of Patrol was current until the 1980s and 170,000 were made.*

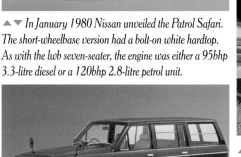

▲▼ In January 1980 Nissan unveiled the Patrol Safari. The short-wheelbase version had a bolt-on white hardtop. As with the lwb seven-seater, the engine was either a 95bhp 3.3-litre diesel or a 120bhp 2.8-litre petrol unit.

▶ The drive for economy became important as the 1980s progressed, and Nissan equipped the Patrol with a new lighter-weight diesel engine, still an in-line 'six' but now of 2.8-litre capacity and having an overhead camshaft. Output was 93bhp, or 115bhp when turbocharged.

▲▶ With the fifth-generation model of 1998 the lines were more graceful but the size was up a notch – which at least meant decent room inside. Thanks to an intercooler, power rose to 130bhp and maximum torque to 193lb ft. Under the more modern skin there were still beam axles (with a diff lock) but at the rear a disconnectable anti-roll bar was fitted.

▲▼ The diesel Patrols sold well in Europe, especially after the first turbo-diesel arrived in 1983, based on the normal 3.3-litre in-line 'six'. Power rose to 110bhp, with maximum torque of 192lb ft at 2000rpm. Both versions used a five-speed gearbox. By now the Nissan name had displaced that of Datsun on the grille.

▼ Nissan targeted the european market, and to give it a leg-up it bought into Motor Iberica, owner of the Spanish marque Ebro. The Patrol was accordingly assembled in Spain, at first under the Ebro name.

▲▼ The fourth-generation Patrol arrived in 1987, carrying the GR ('Grand Raid') badge. The profile was largely unchanged but the flared arches gave the Patrol a more muscular look. At the same time the Nissan's size ballooned, especially in the case of the long-wheelbase model.

▲▼ In 2000, to adapt to the requirements of customers and to meet emissions legislation, Nissan abandoned the traditional six-cylinder engine in favour of a big twin-cam 'four' with four valves per cylinder and direct injection; output was 158bhp.

▲ The 50th birthday of the Patrol was appropriately celebrated with this luxurious range-topping Super Safari with a 280bhp 4.8-litre petrol engine and a four-speed automatic transmission.

Mitsubishi: the oldest of them all

▲ *The first 4x4 in the world? But the Mitsubishi PX33 of 1934 never made it to production.*

▼ *From 1948 until the 1980s Mitsubishi made the CJ3A Jeep under licence. This gave ideas to the other main Japanese marques.*

The triple-diamond marque has quite a history, and one that stands out for two reasons in particular. Firstly, it can be considered to have made the first 4x4 ever, even ahead of the Jeep. Well, perhaps that's labouring the point a little, but the fact remains that even if the car in question never made it to production, it was, back in 1934, the world's first four-wheel-drive civilian vehicle. Built at the request of the Japanese government, four examples of the PX33 were constructed, including a diesel version, and were put through a severe testing regime before receiving government approval. Unfortunately other ventures took priority, above all the manufacture of buses and lorries, which was much more lucrative for the Mitsubishi concern.

The second reason is that in early post-war Japan the Willys Jeep was much envied, for its efficiency and its simplicity – and it was Mitsubishi that secured the contract to make the CJ3A Jeep under licence. This Jeep with the triple-diamond badge was soon very popular, and led to a riposte from Nissan and Toyota, resulting in the creation of their own 4x4 brands.

Yet in Japan the 4x4 remained very much a utility vehicle – not least when Japan was still rebuilding itself economically and didn't allow itself much leisure time. Equally to the point, Mitsubishi found its hands tied, when it came to evolving its 4x4s, by the alliance – advantageous as it was – with the makers of the Jeep. The only option was to start from scratch and come up with a wholly new vehicle. Pushed forward by the booming economy of the 1970s, with paid holidays and the growth of the leisure industry, Mitsubishi struck out, and in 1978 displayed the prototype Pajero – Shogun for the British – at that year's Tokyo Motor Show.

▲ *The first Pajero appeared as a prototype at the 1978 Tokyo show. It was judged to be too close to the Jeep in concept.*

▼ *Another strand of development was the Mitsubishi pick-up, which was especially successful in the US. Voted 'Pick-up of the Year' in 1979, a year later it became available with 4wd: the first of the all-wheel-drive L200s had been born.*

▲ *The definitive Pajero/Shogun appeared at the 1981 Tokyo show, as a three-door estate or canvas-backed pick-up, on a short-wheelbase chassis.*

▲ *It was in 1983 that the Shogun really took off, with the arrival of the long-wheelbase five-door – the wheelbase was 106in, against 92.5in for the swb model. Power came from either a 2.6-litre petrol engine or a 2.3-litre turbo-diesel.*

◄ *With Mitsubishi's image in Japan closely associated with Jeep, the company decided to make a name for itself in competition. It was third time lucky in the 1985 Paris–Dakar, which Patrick Zaniroli won in his Shogun.*

▲ The first Shoguns had independent front suspension by torsion bars and a leaf-sprung live back axle; by 1988 a V6 petrol engine was available, developing 145bhp, and the turbo-diesel – now a 2.5-litre – had gained an intercooler.

▼ The second-generation Shogun received a longer wheelbase (by 2.75in on the swb and 1.2in on the lwb), and the rear suspension went over to coil springs for the live back axle.

▼ In Japan, meanwhile, you could buy this Pajero Mini; available from 1994, it had a 660cc engine. The Shogun itself now used either a 2.8-litre 125bhp turbo-diesel or a 194bhp 3.5-litre V6.

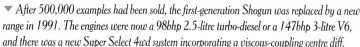

▼ After 500,000 examples had been sold, the first-generation Shogun was replaced by a new range in 1991. The engines were now a 98bhp 2.5-litre turbo-diesel or a 147bhp 3-litre V6, and there was a new Super Select 4wd system incorporating a viscous-coupling centre diff.

▼ The L200 was available in 2wd and 4wd forms, but the twin-cab 4x4 was the choice for many leisure buyers. With an 85bhp 2.5-litre turbo-diesel, performance was respectable.

▶ The Shogun Pinin was a derivative of the earlier Pajero Junior. Designed and built in Italy, by Pininfarina (hence the name), it was 12ft 3in long – or 13ft 3in in five-door form. Power came from 1.8-litre and 2-litre direct-injection petrol engines.

▲ The L200 was restyled in 1996 to take on a more leisure-orientated look. It kept on top of its market-leadership with a 1999 facelift, and in 2001 its engine was up-gunned to 115bhp.

▼ With the Pajero Evolution, of which only 3500 were made, all right-hand-drive, Mitsubishi was the first 4x4 maker to build a homologated off-roader specifically intended for competition. Developing 265bhp, it had only one aim: the Paris-Dakar.

▼ The Shogun Sport of 1998 was originally built for the US market and has a more sporting and less brick-like body. Power comes from a 114bhp 2.5-litre turbo-diesel with manual transmission or a 168bhp 3-litre petrol V6 with automatic gearbox.

▲ The third-generation Shogun of 2000 discarded its separate chassis for a monocoque body, while suspension went over to an all-independent set-up using coil springs all-round. For the UK market either a 4-cylinder 3200cc turbo-diesel (158bhp) or a 3497cc V6 petrol engine (200bhp) are used in the current version.

The explosion of the 4x4 market

▲ *Back in 1983 the Toyota Land Cruiser was still an all-leaf-sprung old bruiser, but that didn't stop Toyota (GB) putting it in front of a Surrey country club for its brochure. One of the other two main shots showed it in front of a smart antique shop – predictable, eh? Off-road images were a few tame shots in a quarry.*

Selling the dream

In the old days it was easy: 4x4s were for people who had mud on their boots or grease under their fingernails. And the market was easy, too: basically it was a Jeep or it was a Land Rover, and even if you were actually running something different, such as an Austin Gipsy in the UK or an International Harvester Scout in the US, people still tended to refer to them as a 'Land Rover' or a 'Jeep', even if they were no such thing.

How things have changed. In Britain the motor of that change was the Range Rover. The Land Rover had been promoted using images of hard-working farmers and contractors; in the evening you changed to your leather-and-wood Rover 95 or your sleek 2000.

Look at an early sales catalogue for the Range Rover and there's a whole new message: this was 'four vehicles in one', you were told, and the images matched workhorse tasks such as surveying with leisure activities such as boating and mountaineering. A new breed had arrived, and soon mud'n'machismo was replaced by healthy outdoor adventure sports and nights on the town.

All the same, you had to remind would-be purchasers of the new-generation off-roaders that while the cars might be suitably civilised they also had tough-as-nails breeding. So a few shots in rocky terrain or up in the hills became – and still are – part of the advertising scenery.

Of course there were some vehicles that couldn't play at being sophisticates, so the brochures continued to major on their functional on-the-farm or down-at-the-quarry character. Who, after all, would want to hack into the West End in a Suzuki SJ or a Daihatsu Fourtrak?

So – where are we today? In a world where the faintly daft word 'lifestyle' has passed into the language, the 4x4 is pitched at healthy 30-something couples with an interest in mountain-biking, skiing, and holidays in south-west France, and you're more likely to see the vehicle photographed on a suburban gravel drive than on a muddy track. Marketing has responded to the market – or should that be the other way round?

▲▶ *In the early Range Rover catalogues, such as this 1972 edition (above), a change had clearly taken place: the car was depicted in use as a leisure vehicle as well as in workhorse roles. This reflected the thinking behind its conception, but also tapped into the different ownership profile for this new breed of vehicle. Mercedes (right) understood, too, photographing its G-Wagen in front of a Dior shop.*

▶ *It was all very manicured-looking, the 1980s UK-market catalogue for the CJ7 Jeep Renegade: gravel drives, neatly-restored converted farm buildings, groomed blonde in heels or in Puffa jacket looking daft with a rifle in her hand. No mud anywhere in sight…*

▼ *By the time of the SJ410, Suzuki in Britain was plugging the hard-top estate as an alternative to an ordinary saloon, whereas the soft-top, ran the brochure copy, 'puts the fun back into weekends'. There was a van version available, and that was naturally enough aimed at the workhorse market.*

◀ *The LJ20 Jimny of the 1970s was a spartan, uncomfortable little thing, and this French-language brochure emphasises the Suzuki's go-anywhere abilities. Shots of gents in tie and jacket wouldn't have been appropriate…*

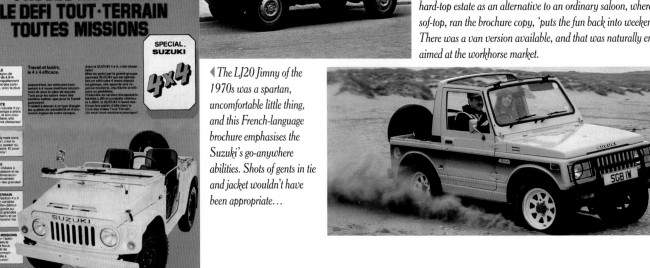

◄ *American marketing people know what is needed: the big outdoors. This 2000 catalogue for the Ford Expedition admirably combines all the requisite clichés: mountains, bubbling streams, desert, camping under a red night sky… The '00 Expedition ran either a 4.6-litre or a 5.4-litre V8 and was available with or without four-wheel drive.*

▶ *In the days when a Land Rover was a Land Rover, and knew its place in the world, this 1980 catalogue was full of shots of the Landie at work – down on the farm, in the quarry, at a construction site, out in the forest. No surprise, then, that a section of the catalogue was devoted to power take-offs…*

◄ *The Toyota BJ40 Land Cruiser didn't need to apologise to anyone when it came to off-road ability, and this French catalogue sends out the appropriate message. Engines were six-cylinder petrol and four-cylinder and six-cylinder diesel.*

▶ *By the 1990s the idea that a 4x4 might never go off the road was becoming accepted. This 1993 Vauxhall Frontera was the perfect transport for a couple of wholesome thirty-somethings to take to their holiday home in the south of France: that seems to be the sub-text here…*

▶ *The Lada Niva was that rare thing in the 1970s, a technically up-to-date soviet vehicle. With its all-coil suspension and permanent 4wd it found a ready market in many European countries; this French catalogue still takes the mud-plugging approach.*

▼ *The original Daihatsu Fourtrak was marketed in England as an alternative to the Land Rover, and was popular for a while, until farmers discovered how badly they rusted. The utilitarian character of the Fourtrak is brought to the fore in this early catalogue.*

▼ *In a land of cheap petrol, a Jeep Cherokee Chief was an ideal tow-car for a US-size caravan. This dated body style was first seen for the 1963 model year, and continued until 1991; suspension was always by leaf springs and rigid axles.*

◄ *The pick-up was again photographed in a leisure setting – athough nobody could doubt the workhorse credentials of these beefy V8-powered (or straight-six) vehicles with their QuadraTrac 4wd. This up-market version has dummy-wood side panels.*

▶ *An oddball from Italy. The Rayton Fissore Magnum was intended as an up-market off-roader, and had a typically Italian interior in wood and leather. Built on a separate chassis, it had Shogun-style torsion-bar independent front suspension and a leaf-spung solid back axle; power came from a VM turbo-diesel or a Lancia/Fiat Volumex-supercharged twin-cam petrol 'four'. If the latter option sounds odd, rest assured: that blown twin-cam pulls like a tractor…*

▲ *This wacky 1981 concept is the Toyota RV-5 'Bird Watching', an interesting take on Toyota's Tercel 4x4 estate launched in 1982. On the production model the rearmost side windows were fixed, rather than being hinged as here.*

▼ *The Jeep origins of this Mahindra Commander hardtop are evident. This is a 2wd version, but 4wd is also available; power comes from a Peugeot diesel. A modernised version of the Jeep-derived Mahindra is the Bolero, which is pitched more at the leisure market and which in its 4wd form has independent front suspension.*

4x4s around the world

Whether for leisure use, army use or business use, the 4x4 is an international phenomenon. In the former Soviet Union and in China, the emphasis has been more on military vehicles, while in France there has been relatively little manufacture of mainstream 4x4s but a steady trickle of 4x4 conversions of existing road cars.

Such vehicles – adaptations of the Renault 4 and 6 and of the Peugeot 504 – have had few production counterparts in France: the only one that springs to mind is Citroën's Méhari 4x4, which with only 1213 made was hardly a success.

In the soft-roader category there have been numerous Subarus over the years, but there was also a very popular but now largely forgotten 4x4 from Toyota, the neat little Tercel 4wd estate introduced in 1982. With its modest dimensions, practical estate bodywork and selectable 4wd, it was the answer to many a leisure-loving driver's prayers, both in Europe and the States.

Less likely to be taken seriously was the Country version of the Golf Mk2. Sitting high on jacked-up suspension and protected by a beefy sumpguard and front and rear bullbars, the Country had permanent 4wd using a viscous central coupling.

Over in Britain the fringe products have been and gone: the Austin Champ was an ill-fated attempt to build a super-Jeep for the British armed forces, while the Austin Gipsy was BMC's challenger for the Land Rover.

Those looking for something rarely encountered elsewhere could turn an eye to India, finally. There, major combine Tata produces the Safari station wagon, and market-leader Mahindra offers various developments of the Willys Jeep, which it began licence-building in the 1940s, and has a smart new SUV in the shape of the Scorpio; additionally Tempo offers its Trax 4x4, a much more rudimentary device now sold under the Judo name.

◀▲ *The Austin Champ (left) began as a Morris, but entered production in 1951 at the Austin factory. It used a four-cylinder Rolls-Royce engine, part of an Army programme of component standardisation. Rather different is the Sinpar 4x4 version of the Renault 4 (above), first available in the sixties.*

▼ *French firm Dangel offered 4wd conversions for the rugged Peugeot 504 – and for the even more rugged 504 pick-up. Still very much in business, the firm can now provide 4x4 versions of the Citroën Berlingo and Peugeot Partner: the 4wd on these is permanent, with a central viscous coupling and lockable front and rear diffs.*

▶ *The plastic-bodied Citroën Méhari 4x4 of 1979–82 had selectable 4wd, a low-range gearbox, and a lockable rear diff. Identification points are the bullbars and the optional but usually specified bonnet-mounted spare wheel.*

	VÉHICULE 4x4 TOUS TERRAINS	CROSS-COUNTRY VEHICLE 4x4	GELÄNDEFAHRZEUG 4x4

Cournil

DIMENSIONS (m)	SCD 14 SCE 14	SCD 24 SCE 24 SCD 28	DIMENSIONS (m)	SCD 14 SCE 14	SCD 24 SCE 24 SCD 28	ABMESSUNGEN (m)
Wheelbase	2.040	2.640	Empattement	2.040	2.540	Radstand
Front track	1.350	1.350	Voie avant	1.350	1.350	Vorderspur
Rear track	1.275	1.275	Voie arrière	1.275	1.275	Hinterachse
Overall length	3.600	4.230	Longueur hors tout	3.600	4.230	Gesamtlänge
Overall width	1.592	1.592	Largeur hors tout	1.592	1.592	Gesamtbreite
Overall height	1.900	1.900	Hauteur hors tout	1.900	1.900	Gesamthöhe
Width between wheel caissons	0.930	0.930	Largeur entre caissons de roues	0.930	0.930	Breite zwischen Radkästen
Effective platform length	1.050	1.670	Longueur de plateau utilisable	1.050	1.670	Länge der Ladefläche
Ground clearance	0.216	0.216	Garde au sol	0.216	0.216	Bodenfreiheit
Front overhang	0.652	0.852	Porte-à-faux avant	0.652	0.652	Vorderer Überstand
Rear overhang	0.908	1.038	Porte-à-faux arrière	0.908	1.038	Hinterer Überstand

WEIGHTS (kg)	SCD 14 SCE 14	SCD 24 SCE 24	SCD 28	MASSES (kg)	SCD 14 SCE 14	SCD 24 SCE 24	SCD 28	GEWICHTE (kg)
Total weight empty	1.490	1.622	1.800	Poids total à vide	1.490	1.622	1.800	Gesamtgewicht leer
Total weight laden	2.360	2.530	2.600	Poids total en charge	2.360	2.530	2.600	Gesamtgewicht beladen
Payload	880	920	870	Charge utile	880	920	870	Nutzlast
Load not to be exceeded				Charge à ne pas dépasser				Nicht zu überschreitende Lasten
Front axle	1.135	1.135	1.135	Essieu AV	1.135	1.135	1.135	Vorderachse
Rear axle	1.590	1.590	1.590	Essieu AR	1.590	1.590	1.590	Hinterachse

FABRIQUÉ EN FRANCE PAR	MANUFACTURED IN FRANCE BY	IN FRANKREICH HERGESTELLT VON

GEVARM
42260 ST-GERMAIN-LAVAL
TEL. (77) 72.39.77
TÉLEX 330990 F

GROUPE **GEVARM** GEVELOT

▲ *The Cournil began life as a Hotchkiss Jeep fitted with a Ferguson tractor diesel, but had evolved into a wholly new vehicle by 1960. Intended for agricultural use above all, it always retained spartan shovel-nosed bodywork. Since 1984 it has been sold first as the Autoland then as the Auverland, and is still available in France. From 1978 until 1996 the Cournil was also manufactured in Portugal, as the UMM.*

▶ *The 1958–68 Austin Gipsy began life with all-independent Flexitor rubber suspension, but latterly went over to conventional leaf springs. The engines were 2.2-litre Austin petrol and diesel units – derived from the old Austin Sixteen 'four'. In all, only 21,208 Gipsys were made – not enough to make Land Rover lose even a wink of sleep.*

◀ *An earlier French 4x4, this is the all-wheel-drive version of Renault's unsuccessful Colorale of 1950–56. In spirit at least a forerunner of the Range Rover, the 4wd Colorale was available as an estate, a canvas-sided two-door van/estate, and a pick-up. The Colorale was intended for colonial and rural use, hence its name.*

◀ *Mahindra's Scorpio was developed on an ultra-tight budget, working closely with component suppliers. The first wholly Indian-designed car, it has been extremely well received, and export sales are now beginning. Most Indian-market sales are of 2wd versions, but Europe will get only 4wd Scorpios.*

▲ *A sensible compromise between an ordinary saloon and an off-roader, or a half-hearted neither-fish-nor-fowl horror? Make up your own mind, but the Golf Country was certainly different, and not totally unreasonable as a proposition in Switzerland, where the author first came across the breed.*

The sport

▶ Hats off to the oldest and the most legendary off-road event of them all: the Rallye des Cimes, which has taken place just about every year since 1951, on the first weekend of September, in the Soule valley deep in the Basque region of France.

▼ The Rallye des Cimes is the key round in the French off-road rally championship, which brings together 12 national rallies – the best-known being the Cidres et Pommiers, the Plaines et Vallées, the Rallye de Gers, and the Ronde de la Fontaine. Shown is the Fouquet buggy which is one of the regular contenders.

▲ Trialling isn't a test of speed, but rather of driving skill, involving the crossing of certain particularly challenging sections of terrain without stopping for more than three seconds and with a penalty for stops of more than two minutes.

▲ Green-laning is a popular pastime, and can be enjoyed in standard vehicles. Beware of wet or wintry conditions, though: you're likely to churn up the track, which won't make you friends with the locals. So be considerate of the environment!

The wonderful world of 4x4 competition

How you use your off-roader depends on where you are in the world. Americans, with plenty of rocks and mountains in their backyard, go 'rock crawling', with jacked-up regular 4x4s or tailor-made tubular-framed buggies. The British, on the other hand, don't have much in the way of rocks to crawl, but they have plenty of soggy scenery and mud, so trials and exploring public by-ways – the latter known as 'greenlaning' – are the most popular forms of 4x4 sport.

There's something for all levels in the British trials world. Road-spec vehicles can compete in the relatively mild 'RTV' ('Road-Taxed Vehicle') class, modified vehicles in the 'CCV' ('Cross-Country Vehicle') class, and the really specialist machinery in the 'Comp-Safari' ('Competition-Safari') class. The British scene is also becoming less insular, with increasing numbers crossing the Channel to participate in continental events.

In France itself, a lot of water has flowed under the bridge since a Basque farmer set up the first off-road trial, the Rallye des Cimes, in 1951. In particular the Paris–Dakar has turned into a veritable nursery for organisers of rallies of this sort. There's the Orpi Maroc Rally; the Rallye de Tunisie, one of the most popular long-distance rallies; the lavish Rallye des Pharaons – Rally of the Pharaohs, in English – which has now been taken over by famous Belgian racing driver Jacky Ickx; the Rallye d'Egypte; and finally the Master Rallye, which, along with the Dakar is the longest of the lot.

Obviously as well as these well-publicised events there are countless off-road events that take place every weekend of the year. Look in the diary pages of a magazine such as *Land Rover Enthusiast*, and you'll find events everywhere from Slovenia to Zimbabwe.

▲◀ The Baja rallies have been going in the States since the beginning of the 1960s. They are several hundred miles long, and real car-breakers, so special vehicles have had to be developed for them. Buggies were the thing for a while, but now the event is dominated by Pro-Trucks and Super-Trucks. The first have to conform to strict rules that make all the vehicles pretty much alike (all with 450bhp or so!) apart from their body, which has to be based on a shell from one of the major manufacturers. Super-Trucks, on the other hand, are less restricted, and can have a power output of up to 1000bhp; their suspension has a crazy amount of travel – up to 43in of movement at the wheel.

▶ Monster Trucks are another ballgame, being stadium entertainment above all. Eliminating rounds lead to a grand finale, with two trucks racing each other across a course comprising obstacles such as a line-up of cars that have to be driven over. In Freestyle events Monster Trucks perform choreographed routines. Needless to say, the whole idea began in the States…

◀▶▶ The Optic 2000 Tunisian Rally (April), the Orpi Maroc Rally (June), the Master Rally (August), the Las Pampas Argentine Rally (September) and the UAE Desert Challenge of Dubai (November) are all FIA-affiliated and count – with the Bajas – towards the World Off-Road Rally Championship, which comprises eight events in total. As can be seen, a wide variety of machinery takes part in these well-sponsored events.

◀▼ The Bajas have had their European counterparts for a good while, and they also count towards the World Championship. There are three of them: the Italian Baja (March), the Telecel Vodafone Baja 1000 (May), and finally the Baja Espana Aragón (July). There's also the non-championship Baja Deutschland that takes place in September.

▶ Pikes Peak is the name of a mountain in Colorado. It's also a stony 12-mile track which climbs the 14,000ft mountain by means of 56 bends. Pikes Peak is the world's best-known hillclimb, and is nicknamed The Race to the Clouds. Ari Vatanen has won in a Dakar-style off-road Peugeot 405, and Michèle Mouton – the only lady winner to date – in an Audi Quattro. The fearsome device shown is the 900bhp Suzuki Side Kick of Nobuhiro Tajima that came second in the 1999 event.

◀ The Berlin–Breslau is unique of its type, and probably one of the toughest off-road rallies. A mix of Camel Trophy and long-distance rally, it puts man and machine to the sternest of tests: 1250 miles of special stages, against the clock, over the most demanding of terrain, to be completed in seven days…

▶ American trials are bound to be something else. The vehicles are modified in the most amazing fashion, to very high standards and at substantial expense. Wild stuff…

▶ *Thierry Sabine died in 1986 in a helicopter accident that also claimed the life of singer Daniel Balavoine, journalist Nathaly Odent, pilot François-Xavier Bag and radio technician Jean-Paul Le Fur.*

▲ *The Mareaux brothers finished second in the car class in this wonderful Sinpar 4wd Renault 4 and did even better in 1982 in a Renault 20, winning the event.*

▼ *It seems incredible today that a VW Iltis could win the Dakar – but these are tough vehicles, and one year they even managed a one-two. This was with the Swedish team of Kotullinski/Luffelman followed by French duo Zanirolli/Colesse – and rally ace Jean Ragnotti bought another Iltis home in fourth place. More would be heard of the name Zaniroli…*

The Dakar from 1979 until 1986

A gentleman by the name of Thierry Sabine

On 26 December 1978, on the Place du Trocadéro in Paris, 170 competitors, in a collection of oddball machinery, gathered almost on the sly before setting off on a 6000-mile race across across Algeria, Niger, Mali, Upper Volta and Senegal. A race that would become one of the most famous in history: the Paris–Dakar.

At the time, this all-French venture was regarded as something of a nutters outing. And yet the chap who'd come up with the idea, Thierry Sabine, had a rock-solid belief in the event. It was taking place in a dead season for sporting stories, in the middle of the French winter, and even if it coincided with the Christmas holidays he was sure that pictures of the desert and of magical adventure-story scenery would be lapped up by the hungry media.

It was a crazy gamble, all the same, even if it paid off. In 1982 there were already 382 lambs to the slaughter. By 1985 that figure had jumped to 568, and in 1988 there was the record number of 603 participants to celebrate the rally's tenth birthday. Today it is one of France's most popular and most media-covered sporting events, up there just behind Formula 1.

It is necessary to go back to those first events to understand that the entrants then really were people apart. Safety measures had nothing in common with what is insisted upon today. The cars were often production models, generally prepared by people who didn't have much experience. You didn't know what you'd find in the various countries, in terms of political instability, ethnic strife, and so on. There were none of the things taken for granted today, such as satellite-navigation, the helicopter-doctor, portable phones, or the distress flare now carried by every competitor. Not only were these things not part and parcel of the event; they were unthinkable at the time. Bear in mind that the only medical vehicles were two simple two-wheel-drive Peugeot 504 estates.

If the event carried on after its hesitant start, despite the lack of the current logistical back-up, this was down to the the mutual respect and spirit of helping each other that was generated among the participants, thanks in part to the feeling that they were more fellow-adventurers than competitors, but thanks also to a man of incredible charisma, whom you'd follow to the ends of the earth. That man was Thierry Sabine.

◀ *The BJ Land Cruiser was another strong challenger for top placings, and thanks to its inherent reliability needed little in the way of preparation. Shown here is Jean-Jacques Ratet.*

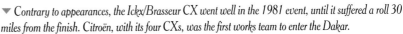

▼ *Contrary to appearances, the Ickx/Brasseur CX went well in the 1981 event, until it suffered a roll 30 miles from the finish. Citroën, with its four CXs, was the first works team to enter the Dakar.*

▲ *A Rolls-Royce on the Dakar? It had to be either bravado or provocation. Whatever it was, you couldn't say that Thierry de Montcorgé and Jean-Christophe Pelletier failed in their bid for publicity on the 1981 event: everyone still talks of their Rolls. Crewe, who hadn't approved the venture, was not impressed…*

▲ *Mercedes also had its moment of glory with the G-Class, Ickx/Brasseur winning the 1983 event. But that year also saw the first appearance of the Shogun, with one winning the production-car class.*

▲ *This neat Lada Niva came third in the 1981 event, with Briavoine at the wheel; it was entered by French Lada importer Poch. In 1986 Lartigue finished fourth in a much more evolved version of the Niva.*
▶ *The first Dakar, in 1979, was won by this Range Rover, of trio Genestier/Thierblaut/Lemordant. Two years later René Metge repeated the exploit.*

▲ *'Zani' at last got his win in 1985, in a Mitsubishi Shogun. He'd been second in 1980 in an Iltis, sixth in 1981 in a Range Rover, seventh the following year, again in a Range Rover, and then second in 1984, still Solihull-mounted and just a forgivable distance behind Metge's winning Porsche.*

▼ *From the moment they appeared, the Porsche 959s dominated the Dakar. René Metge, partnered by Dominique Lemoyne, won in 1984, with Ickx/Brasseur sixth, after electrical troubles; Metge and Ickx went on to come in 1–2 in the 1986 event.*

▲ *The diversity of cars entered, the need to cross a river by hand-winched ferry, the magnificent equatorial forest – Africa quite simply has a magical ambience.*

▲ The eleventh Dakar was the eleventh event for the Mareaux brothers (driver Bernard shown), who had been the first to sign up for the first Paris-Dakar of 1979; for the 1989 event they were in a Shogun.

▼ One of two Lada Samara protos on the 1990 event, driven by Jérôme Rivière, who had come in tenth in 1988 in a Toyota.

The Peugeot era: domination

The arrival of Peugeot literally changed the ground rules of endurance off-road rallying. There was the Dakar before Peugeot and the Dakar with Peugeot. Even if Porsche in its time gave a foretaste of what the event would become in terms of ever-mounting budgets and forever-increasing power outputs, even if there was subsequently the fear that Mitsubishi, so overcome by its wins, might exercise a stranglehold on the rally, nothing could compare with the effect of the arrival of the Peugeot armada in 1987.

Leading the team was Ari Vatanen, fresh from the World Rally Championship. It would be his first entry in the Dakar, and also his first victory…of many! Vatanen didn't take long to understand the disciplines, even if he was last at the end of the preliminary leg after losing a wheel. All the same he had some stiff internal opposition, in the shape of the Kenyan Shekhar Mehta, who knew Africa well (as you might expect) and had no fear of the mind-boggling power of the 205 Turbo 16. But the desert doesn't have properly mapped-out roads, and in the end it was Zaniroli in a Range Rover who put in a marvellous performance to come in second.

The next year was a landmark year. First 'The Flying Madman', Juha Kankhunen, made his appearance. Then 1988 was also the start of all those Dakar 'stories', with that year seeing the 'theft' of Vatanen's 405, later re-found, forcing him to abandon the event. It was also the year that Hubert Auriol made the move to four wheels, and the year that Stéphane Peterhansel and Jutta Kleinschmidt made their debut, on two wheels – not that the significance of their arrival was grasped at the time. Finally, it was also the blackest year of the Dakar, with the death of a 10-year-old girl, two fellow-competitors, a motorcyclist, and two journalists, not to mention the paralysis after an accident of talented motorcyclist André Malherbe.

In 1989 Vatanen, in spite of an unfortunate incident on the preliminary leg when he executed a superb roll-over in front of an appreciative TV audience, added another victory to his tally. But history will also not forget the ill-thought-out way of settling the result, again in front of the television cameras, when Jean Todt, Peugeot's team manager, decided who'd be the winner on the toss of a coin. This wouldn't be Todt's last misjudgement. Still, to make one forget, the Peugeot team scored a brilliant 1–2–3 the next year, proof of their breathtaking supremacy.

▼ The competitors and the TV-watching public discovered a country of whose splendour they had been unaware; but then Libya is better known for its head of state…

◀ Ickx turned his back on Peugeot in 1990 and returned to one of his first loves, fielding a Porsche-engined Samara proto; but it couldn't see off the Peugeots.

▶ Gilbert Sabine, Thierry's father, took over the reins in 1987, after the death of his son. He was supported by René Metge, who was yet to get involved in rally organisation on his own account.

▲ Jean-Pierre Fontenay had come a long way by 1990, working his way up from mechanic to co-pilot to driver, to the point where he now had a works Mitsubishi drive. And his story wouldn't end there…

▲ It was a difficult era for Mitsubishi, which found itself always following in Peugeot's dust trails. But the Dakar became very popular in Japan, all the same, thanks to Japanese driver Shinosuka, who had four top-five placings in this period.

▼ This Mitsubishi PX33, supposedly a replica of Mitsubishi's 1933 4wd prototype, finished 31st in the hands of Papy Jaussaud.

▶ In 1990 Jean-Jacques Ratet repeated the magnificent sixth placing he'd achieved in 1988. Faithful to the event, he has entered almost all the Dakars since 1979, always behind the wheel of a Toyota. Guess what he used to win the production-car class in 2002…

▼ Pierrot de Mostaganem, alias Lartigue, pokes the nose of his works Shogun forward. Perhaps a little too fiery at first, he ended up showing that an 'African hand' could go as fast, if not faster, than a regular rally driver, Finnish or not…

▼ A 1–2–3 for Peugeot in 1990! The marque could step back, its head held high, as could team manager Jean Todt, leaving the field to Citroën and Guy Fréquelin.

▲ In the 1988 event Vatanen in the superb new 405 T16 was expected to win, but in the end it was Juha Kankhunen, the World Rally Champion, who claimed victory, at the wheel of a 205 for the first time. Top rally drivers got the hang of the Dakar pretty quickly. Beside Kankhunen in this shot is Guy Fréquelin, who suffered a few problems along the way.

▼ After a nasty fall from his motorcycle (two broken ankles) the year before, when he was leading the rally, Hubert Auriol began a new career on four wheels, setting off in an astonishing 2wd buggy. He wasn't stacking the cards in his favour…

◀ Endurance rallies are a real melting-pot, with drivers coming from all spheres of the sport. Patrick Tambay is a perfect example, the ex-F1 driver finishing third in a Range Rover on his first Dakar and repeating the exploit the next year in a works Shogun.

43

▶ *In passing the baton to Citroën, Peugeot didn't really change things: Vatanen was still untouchable, winning again in 1991.*

▲▼ *A new Mitsubishi prototype put the Japanese marque on equal terms with Citroën and demonstrated the turn of speed of some old hands that the malicious had started to say were past their best. Lartigue and Fontenay finished second and third, respectively, in the 1991 event.*

▼ *Hubert Auriol won several stages and finished fifth in 1991 in his Lada prototype.*

▲ *Gérard Sarrazin (here with Gérard Troublé) is inextricably linked with Toyota. In his big Land Cruiser he has worked wonders, but back in Japan they haven't wanted to get more involved.*

The Dakar from 1991 until 1996
The Citroën-Mitsubishi era: mass attack!

This was when Peugeot made way for Citroën, but of course it was still the same team; the first year of the period in question also saw the even stronger involvement of Mitsubishi, with the arrival of new prototypes that could do battle on more equal terms with the Peugeots-turned-Citroëns. The Japanese team, despite six stage victories, didn't manage to put Vatanen off his stroke, and 1991 saw the master chalk up a remarkable fourth victory.

The following year was a massive gamble: the Dakar wouldn't go to Dakar, but would carry on to the Cape, 7722 miles down at the bottom of Africa. That was really chancing it, given the political turmoil that so often wracked – and still wracks – the continent. Another novelty was the arrival of satellite navigation.

Mitsubishi wrapped things up nicely, with a 1–2–3 in the general classification, with team newcomer Hubert Auriol leader of the pack, nine years after his last Dakar on two wheels. Until 2004 he was the only person to have won on both two wheels and four. The next year Bruno Saby secured a second victory for Mitsubishi, in his first year with the team, with Dominique Serieys as his co-driver.

The 1994 event was dominated by a huge erg, or sea of sand, on the Atar–Nouadhibou stage, which cost many teams dearly. The Citroëns decided to turn back, and risk being penalised. The Mitsubishis, after 36 hours of struggling, managed to get through, and the Saby-Serieys and Fintenay-Musmara pairings became real heroes in the process. But in the end they were outside the time limit, and ended up being disqualified. Fenouil threw in the towel as the new organiser, and was replaced the following year by Hubert Auriol, who duly hung up his helmet.

Victory in the 1994 event went to Pierre Lartigue, as it did in the two subsequent Dakars – giving Vatanen something to chew on, one feels sure. He wasn't able to build on this hat-trick, though, as in 1997 the prototype class was banned, bringing with it the withdrawal of the Citroën team.

▶ *Auriol fought to the end against Erwin Weber to secure his first victory on four wheels and for Mitsubishi, in the fantastic Paris–Cape event of 1992 – in which the team managed a magnificent 1–2–3.*
▼ *André Dessoude, a former Dakar driver turned Nissan preparer, had more luck with the Terrano (Pathfinder in some markets) he entered for the talented Jean Boucher: it finished eighth, and first in the T1 class in 1991.*

▲ The narrow-body ZX Rallye Raid proto gave way to a wide-bodied evolution, in a new red livery, for 1993.

◀ ▲ Pierre Lartigue fell out with Mitsubishi and turned to Citroën. His ZX just seemed to get better and better, and he scored one second place before winning three Dakars on the trot, in 1994, 1995 and 1996.

▼ ▶ Bruno Saby couldn't repeat his 1993 victory, despite a new Mitsubishi T3 prototype, given the might of the Citroën team.

▲ People were beginning to take notice of Jean-Louis Schlesser and his buggy: in 1993 he finished 14th, still running with no co-driver.

▼ Vatanen was maybe beginning to doubt himself. He wasn't to win any more Dakars – but with four victories he is still the person who has won the event more times than anyone else.

▲ The dream come true! Jean-Pierre Fontenay and Bruno Musmara were fourth in 1995, third in 1996…and then, two years later, it happened: Fontenay drove his Mitsubishi into first place, dedicating the victory to his former co-driver.

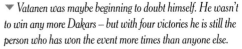

▼ Masuoka saved the honour of the Japanese team in 1994, the year in which the three Mitsubishi protos were stuck in the sand and were disqualified. He finished fourth, and first in the T2 class – yet still people failed to appreciate his talent!

▲ The king of the T1 class is Thierry De Lavergne. Driving the Dessoude Terrano, he not only regularly wins the T1 class but also usually finds himself in the top ten overall.

▲ *Four, three, two, one…Victory! That's what Jean-Pierre Fontenay managed, in that order, over four Dakars in a row, ending with his well-deserved win on the 20th event. He's still one of the fastest drivers.*

▼ *Even if the race wasn't fought as such, it was Shinosuka who came first in the 1989 Dakar, after Mitsubishi had given team instructions for the finishing order of its cars, to avoid a fratricidal battle between its drivers.*

▲▶▼ *Lots of time, lots of work, lots of skill…and lots of different buggies before Jean-Louis Schlesser reached the top of the tree – an achievement he owes only to his own efforts.*

The Dakar from 1997 to date
Schlesser against Goliath !

The 19th Dakar saw both a change of rules and of organiser (*bonjour*, Hubert Auriol!) for what was now the Dakar-to-Dakar, run in a loop starting and ending in the Senegalese capital: prototypes were henceforth only allowed in the case of private teams. Citroën felt constrained to withdraw, and Mitsubishi had the field to itself, and duly romped home in the top four places, with a finishing order, led by Shinosuka, which had already been established by mid-event. Jean-Pierre Fontenay and Bruno Saby were second and third respectively, with Masuoka coming in fourth. The only resistance to the Mitsubishi steamroller came from Jean-Louis Schlesser, with his buggy, but he was forced to abandon with a mechanical problem. In another buggy Jutta Kleinschmidt came to the notice of the public with a first in the special class – the first time a woman had won this class. From this point on in the history of the Dakar, it has always been pretty much the same actors, following the same script, who have been mercilessly fighting it out amongst themselves for the top prizes.

For the event's 20th birthday – with its memorable stages from Zouerat to Gao – it was Jean-Pierre Fontenay who received the laurels, immediately dedicating his richly-deserved victory to his long-time co-driver and friend Bruno Musmara, who had died two years earlier. Schlesser, the only one to put up a fight against the Mitsubishis, finished fifth, and was obviously well in the groove – as he'd prove in style the following year. Another pointer for the future was that Jutta Kleinschmidt finished third.

The new millennium was celebrated with an historic route from Dakar to the pyramids of Egypt – a high-speed itinerary which benefited Schlesser and his high-performance buggy, enabling him to reach Cairo ahead of Peterhansel in his Méga. This was the Dakar that will be remembered, too, for its fantastic logistics after the organisers had to move the entire rally by air-lift, in the middle of a stage, as the result of a terrorist threat.

Then there was the 2001 event, the first won by a woman, Jutta Kleinschmidt, and the year 2002, with the arrival of the very promising Nissan pick-ups and the splendid victory of Hiroshi Masuoka – a feat he repeated the following year as part of a Mitsubishi 1-2-3. The 2004 event was also won by Mitsubishi, and made victor Stéphane Peterhansel only the second driver ever to have triumphed in the Dakar on both two wheels and four.

▲ *The Nissan pick-ups were welcome newcomers on the 2002 Dakar, and were fully competitive, even if they weren't as highly tuned as they could have been. Here Peterhansel gives it some…*

▼ *It had been a long time without a Toyota joining in the party, but in the 2002 event Jean-Jacques Ratet took his Araco Toyota to first place in the production-car class and ninth overall.*

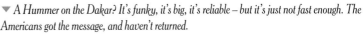

A Hummer on the Dakar? It's funky, it's big, it's reliable – but it's just not fast enough. The Americans got the message, and haven't returned.

▲ Mitsubishis on the beach. With Jean-Louis Schlesser having changed to a new turbo-diesel that proved too fragile, Mitsubishi had nine vehicles in the top ten in 2002.

▼ Jutta Kleinschmidt succeeded in winning the 2001 event, and in 2002 she proved she was as fast as the best. In 2003 she joined the newly-formed VW team, but had a disappointing '04 event, it being down to team-mate Bruno Saby to show the Touareg's potential with a sixth place.

▼ It didn't take long for the Méga to prove what it was capable of: with Stéphane Peterhansel at the wheel it was pure dynamite! Result: second place in 2000.

▼ Thierry Delavergne has been a multiple winner of the marathon class, and he was also a class winner in the old T2 category, still in a Nissan. He is fast and consistent.

▼ Maybe Bruno Saby didn't make the right choice with his Ford Protruck. Although he won the Optic 2000 Tunisian Rally with the Ford, it never shone in his hands.

▼ The Mad Skiier, as they call Luc Alphand, isn't on the Dakar just to look pretty, so it's a shame his Kangoo doesn't really cut it.

▲ Grégoire de Mevius got fed up waiting for Nissan to enter the Dakar officially and so he switched to the BMW X-Raid team. Here he is in action on the 2002 Orpi Maroc rally, the X5's maiden event and one which promised well for the future.

▶ A big name for his qualities of endurance and tenacity, J-P Strugo has won the marathon class in a Mitsubishi and then in a Mercedes ML. He's taken the odd risk along the way…

▲ The Mercedes MLs of the Georges Groines team managed the feat of pulling off a win in the production-car class without factory support. At the wheel here is another ex-motorcyclist (and former World Champion off-road biker), Thierry Magnaldi.

The Dakar: playground of the stars!

Ever since the second Dakar, two celebrities have been part of the scenery: Henri Pescarolo, the former Formula 1 driver and three-times Le Mans victor, and actor Yves Regnier, famous for his role on French TV as Inspector Moulin. Between them these two comrades-in-arms have launched the Dakar fashion among motor-sport and entertainment celebs. Not that they set out to do this: at the time there was hardly sufficient media coverage of the event for them to be accused of courting publicity. That's something you couldn't necessarily say about some of those who have followed…

You couldn't accuse Jacky Ickx of publicity-seeking, though. The famous Belgian racing driver has joined in as an entrant at all different levels. At first he was a privateer with Claude Brasseur in a superb Porsche 4x4 and then in a Mercedes G280 in which the duo came home first. Then he was a works driver in a Citroën ZX, only to see his 1989 victory snatched away when first place was decided on the toss of a coin, and Ari Vatanen was pronounced the winner. Finally he was back to

being a privateer, in a Land Cruiser, passing on his enthusiasm to his daughter Vanina. After all that, how could anyone doubt his good faith?

The Dakar has become such a media event that in any case the most talented drivers, whether regulars or not, have rapidly become real stars. Some make the front pages, because of who they are; others labour away in the shadows, busting a gut simply to get to the finish and see the banks of the famous Lac Rose in Dakar. The old guard, meanwhile, have largely disappeared from view, often moving on to the organisational side, either for the Dakar or for their own events, as in the case of Hubert Auriol, Cyril Neveu, René Metge, Patrick Zaniroli and Fenouil.

At the end of the day, though, there's what is always in the background, trampled on by the Dakar and indifferent to it for the rest of the year, if you believe the detractors. That something that for most entrants, once they've sampled it, brings them back year after year, like a drug. If there's a real star of the Dakar, it's Africa itself, the brightest star of them all.

▲ Hubert Auriol is the current organiser of the Dakar. As one of only two people to have won both on two wheels and on four, who better to run it? Before hanging up his gloves he was also the only person to have done every Dakar – almost always with a smile on his face.

◀ Jean-Pierre Fontenay arrived by the back door. But this modest young man is fair bursting with sheer gumption and has climbed the ladder as if in a fairy story, progressing from mechanic to co-driver to driver, before scooping the 20th Dakar. Sporty and hungry for victory, he's not going to stop there, you can be sure.

▼ Sunrise, the morning after a marathon leg of the event, and when everyone had been obliged to sleep rough. Smiling for the camera are Luc Alphand and Vanina Ickx: no celebrity-luvvie flouncing around for these two!

◀ Jean-Louis Schlesser is a case apart, with an impressive and varied CV that includes two world sports-prototype championships, a spell in F1 (with a sixth place his best result), and a win in the Trophée Andros superfinal. As an off-roader he has won four World Championships, two Dakars, and countless other rallies. What's more, he uses a car he's designed himself.

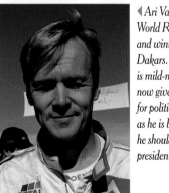

◀ Ari Vatanen, 1981 World Rally Champion and winner of four Dakars. As talented as he is mild-mannered, he has now given up motor-sport for politics. If he's as good as he is behind the wheel, he should soon be president of Finland…

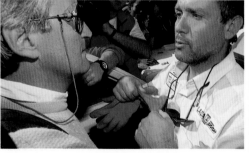

▲ Patrick Tambay (left) hasn't yet won a Dakar, but in 1987 the former F1 driver came along for a bit of relaxation and finished third; here he's in conversation with Lada team manager Hugues de Chaunac.

▼ Two Mitsubishi hotshoes chew the cud. Stéphane Peterhansel (left), three times winner of the motorcycle class, won on four wheels in 2004; here he is chatting with 2002 and 2003 winner Hiroshi Masuoka.

▲ Pierre Lartigue has a crazy talent; he's another one of those who don't owe their success to anybody but themselves, and who came up the hard way. With a dab hand at the wheel and a dogged determination, he has won three Dakars – and certainly the most difficult three.

▲ Jutta Kleinschmidt began endurance rallying on motorbikes, and showed the men the way home on a special stage of the Rallye des Pharaons. She was soon showing she had what it took on four wheels. Taken under Schlesser's wing, she had the best mentor in the business, but obviously wanted to strike out on her own – which she did successfully, with her win in 2001.

▼ Bruno Saby, caught concentrating just before the start of a special stage, when he was a works driver for Mitsubishi. In world rally championships Saby was unbeatable on tarmac, and he wasn't fazed by the Dakar's sands, either, winning the 1993 event which was one of the hardest-fought and most challenging.

◀ He did the Adidjan–Nice in 1977 on a motorbike and got lost in the Libyan desert. Found in the nick of time, he returned to France in thrall to the desert, and with a single idea in his head: a race to Dakar across the never-ending sands. It would be 'a challenge for those who set off, and a dream for those who stay at home'; that's as true now as it was 25 years ago. Thanks again, Thierry Sabine.

◀ A living legend and one of the Dakar pioneers, four-times Le Mans winner Henri Pescarolo fell in love with the event when he entered for the first time in 1980. His hardest Dakar of all was the 1998 edition, which he did in a 2wd Protruck. Although it was one of the toughest Dakars, he managed to finish, and he's even been back since!

▲ Patrick Zaniroli works alongside Hubert Auriol as sporting director of the Dakar. He was a talented driver himself, and won the 1985 event – the first victory for Mitsubishi. He has also organised the Rallye de l'Atlas.

◀ Philippe Wambergue has driven for most makes, with the exception of Mitsubishi. Wherever he goes, he wins plaudits for being a big-hearted and honourable man with real ability behind the wheel.

◀ From left to right are Shinozuka, Fontenay, Kleinschmidt and Masuoka, training before the 2002 Dakar. Between them they account for five victories on the event, and that year they went on to scoop the top four places on the rally.

▲ What a super photo! Brasseur and Ickx camping out, in complete simplicity, and enjoying an evening apple, on the 1984 Dakar.

▼ Along with Jean-Christophe Pelletier, Cyril Neveu organises the Maroccan and Tunisian rallies – and has run the latter for more than a decade. He has been motorcycle winner of the Dakar five times.

◀ Fenouil is a former journalist on Moto-Journal, and fell in love with Africa as if he'd been born there. He was a pioneer of endurance rallies with his Côte d'Azur to Côte d'Ivoire raid, ancestor of the Dakar.

▼ When he took part in the 2002 event Johnny Halliday (left) generated plenty of publicity – as befits someone who is one of France's biggest stars. But the rock singer, a sort of French Jagger-cum-Elvis, has now done two Dakars, and has set up the Master Rallye, so he's no greenhorn.

Adventure

Right from the start, exploration and the discovery of the unknown were foremost; here the Trophy is in Papua New Guinea, in 1982.

▲ *The first Camel Trophy, in 1980, was run in Jeeps, in Brazil, six cars leaving Germany for the Americas.*

▲ *The Range Rover was the second vehicle to be used, and initiated the tie-in with Land Rover that lasted until the end; this is Sumatra, during the 1981 event.*
▼ *In 1983 it was the turn of Zaire, and of the 88in Land Rover as chosen vehicle. This was its only appearance, as the following year saw the arrival of the new-generation 90 and 110 models.*

The Camel Trophy: a terrific story

Camel Trophy. Two words which are enough to set more than a few people dreaming! With nineteen editions to its credit, it was one of the most envied events in the world, for those who'd have liked to have been part of it. But what was it?

In essence the Camel Trophy was an international off-road endurance trial in which man had to face down a natural world that wasn't always hospitable and was sometimes downright hostile, in order to probe his own limits. Taking place each year in a different country, this great adventure allowed participants with the same passion to discover landscapes, peoples and cultures while putting to the test their ability to cope with each other's personalities. Everyone had to dig deep into each others' physical and mental resources to overcome all the obstacles and get to the finish.

After having passed the first hurdle of a draconian paper selection process, followed by tests on the ground (both national and international), two-person teams – one per country – were then despatched to far-flung countries, each more fantastic than the next. Brazil, Sumatra, Papua New Guinea, Zaire, The Amazon, Borneo, Australia, Madagascar, Sulawesi, Siberia, Tanzania and Burundi, Guyana, Argentina and Chile, Belize, Samoa – so many magnificent and unknown destinations where each time some 1000 miles had to be covered in expedition-equipped 4x4s! From the Jeep to the Freelander, via the gamut of Land Rovers (Defender, Range Rover and Discovery), the Camel Trophy has pitched man against machine in the toughest possible way.

The Camel Trophy always remained an adventure on a personal level, made up of a multitude of discoveries and encounters. It was a real legend among global adventuring, and more's the shame that it all ended in 2000 with the holding of the last event.

▲ *Brazil was the 1984 venue. For its second trans-Amazon event the Trophy took up where it had left off in 1980, at a place the Indians called 'The Land that God hasn't Finished Creating'.*

▲ *Siberia in 1990 saw the first appearance of the Discovery. The contestants had to cover more than 1000 miles, during the raspoutitsa, the Russian post-winter thaw that had once bogged down Napoleon's Grand Army.*

▼ *For 1992 it was Guyana. To cope with the terrain the Discoverys had a 19½-gallon fuel tank, an Africa-spec air filter with raised-up intake, a roll-cage, additional lights, and an electric winch.*

▲ *'The Green Hell' – that's what the contestants called Borneo, to which the Trophy returned in 1993. This was the first time a train was used to get the cars from one point to another on the island.*

▲ *With their five-door Discoveries, complete with 2.5-litre direct-injection diesel and five-speed gearbox, the contestants had the wherewithal in 1994 to cross three countries (Argentina, Paraguay and Chile) for the first time – roughly 1500 miles in 19 days.*

▲ *1994 saw a new guiding idea for the Trophy: ecology and inter-action with local people. Thus the participants took time off while in Argentina to build a research centre for the University of Salta.*

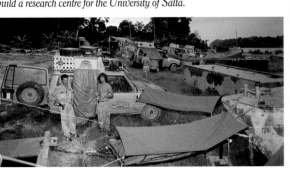

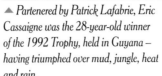

▲ *Partenered by Patrick Lafabrie, Eric Cassaigne was the 28-year-old winner of the 1992 Trophy, held in Guyana – having triumphed over mud, jungle, heat and rain.*

▲ *An important development took place in 1994: the arrival of the first woman competitor. But 30-year-old Karine Duret was as handy with an adjustable as with a winch.*

▲ *For the 1995 Trophy, in central America, one of the stars was a young Spanish lady called Belen; she survived to the end of the 1000-mile event.*

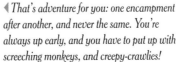

▲ *Iain Chapman, an eminent Camel Trophy personality: he was the man on the ground, responsible for the route, the reconnaissances and the smooth running of the selection process and the expeditions themselves.*

◀ *That's adventure for you: one encampment after another, and never the same. You're always up early, and you have to put up with screeching monkeys, and creepy-crawlies!*

▲ *The year is 1994, and this impressive convoy kicking up the sand is crossing the world's most arid desert, the Atacama in Chile – the first time the Trophy took in desert terrain.*

▲ *In 1996 the Trophy again used Discoveries, to cross the Indonesian part of Borneo, from Balikpapan to Pontianak in the west. It was some challenge, with bridges having to be built, and some serious winchmanship.*

▲ *Something new for 1997: the Mongolia of Ghensis Khan. Time was split between exploring the country and the rigours of the competition itself.*

▼ *For 1998 there was a change of rhythm and of scenery, with Freelanders being used to explore Tierra del Fuego.*

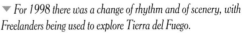

▶ *The Atacama desert in Chile is the world's most arid, with a lunar landscape of devastating beauty. For six days the convoy looked as if it was on an African rally, as they rolled along in clouds of sand.*

▲ *The uncrossable tracks in Guyana didn't dent the moral of the troops: each tent was pitched with military precision in a magnificent setting. The green savannah contrasts with the thick jungle experienced up until then.*
▼ *Here the Camel Trophy caravan had to face up to the snares and delusions of Borneo. The rafts never saw as much use as on this event: in the centre of the island the only way of getting about was by river.*

▼ *In all 20 teams crossed Mongolia, in all weathers, leaving from the capital, Ulan Bator, and returning there via the Gobi desert.*

Camel Trophy: the travel makes it

With more than 30 countries crossed, thousands of miles travelled across sand, mud and snow, and thousands of encounters with local peoples, the Camel Trophy will always be remembered as one of the most wonderful voyages of adventure ever devised. It was a real journey to the ends of the earth, involving hundreds of men – and women – and their 4x4s.

Some years were quite extraordinary, such as 1982, when there was the amazing encounter with the Papuans in Papua New Guinea, something nobody is ever likely to forget. With the natives not sure whether the teams were chasers of monsters or were evil spirits, the Camel Trophy lived through an adventure that really was unique.

That's the other side of the Trophy – that constant discovery of the beauties of the world and its different cultures, that mission of bringing native tribes something new, a taste of the modern age, but also aid when they needed it. In 1993, for example, the Camel Trophy teams crossed the state of Sabah, in the north of Borneo, to get to the 'Lost World', where their task was to build a base camp for ecological researchers.

Whether in the jungle, in the snow, in the Siberian steppes, in sand, or whatever, the Camel Trophy has experienced every range of temperature, every type of drought, and lived through every imaginable change of scenery.

◀ *Here's a typical example of the difficulties encountered in Borneo: the magnificent countryside always hid a trap.*
▶ *The 850ft drop at these waterfalls in Guyana was a magnificent sight. With a deafening din and an unbelievable cascade of white foam, the waters crashed down in front of the expedition's eyes. At last the Tapui plateau was surrendering the secret of the oldest rock formations in the world...*

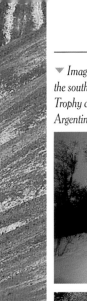

▼ *Imagine yourself at the other end of the world, at Ushuaia, the southernmost town on the planet… In 1998 the Camel Trophy crossed the plains of Patagonia, from Chile to Argentina, before reaching the glaciers of Tierra del Fuego.*

▲ *Crowded in by the rocky mountain escarpments, the Camel Trophy convoy will find a way through, you can bet on it. This starkly beautiful terrain in Chile was remarkable for its utter tranquillity.*

▲ *The 1995 event among the Mayas was the most enriching in the Trophy's history, with an archaeological mission at the Maya site of Rio Azul in Mexico, complete with digs and cartographic work.*

▲ *On the Camel Trophy that famous French word fraternity is no empty expression! Working together was what it was all about, on this 1996 crossing of Borneo.*

▲ *At the heart of the action, thick in the mysterious and impenetrable jungles of Borneo! You couldn't put a foot wrong if you wanted to get through this luxuriant and ensnaring vegetation. This first crossing of the island by 4x4 left the competitors with incredible memories.*

▲ *Whatever the weather, the Camel Trophy vehicles had to eat up the miles without blanching, across terrain that was astonishing and unpredictable. Hot one day, cold the next: you could never be sure.*

▲ *In 1993 the 16 national teams crossed Sabah, in north Borneo, to reach the 'Lost World'. To get there, all means were good! The reward was scenery to take your breath away.*
◀ *In the desert it's tough taking in the scenery and keeping the vehicle rolling without ending up in trouble. In the end, it's the travel experience that is more important than the competitive element…*

▲ *Still in Borneo, where a bridge had to be rebuilt: crossing had to be carried out with great care.*
▶ *You can never talk enough about those sunrises and sunsets, that glorious light that illuminated the 4x4s as they made their way onwards. Life can't be that bad when you're alone in the desert with nothing but the moaning of the wind!*

▲ *The hellhole of Borneo continues to exert its power. The sheer humidity in the tropical rainforest and the monsoon rains caused some more vulnerable tracks to be washed away before the convoy was able to get there.*

Camel Trophy: you said extreme?

Sometimes the best and worst of times co-exist. In the case of the Camel Trophy that is doubly true. Some places are more difficult to reach than others, are more inhospitable, or more demanding to get through. Take Borneo, otherwise known as the Green Hell, as an example. This was 1985, and the Camel convoy was stuck in the middle of a river. The vehicles covered 300 yards in 24 hours. It was finally a helicopter that transported the 4x4s ten miles further on, so they could continue on their way. Never had the Land Rovers come closer to being amphibious, whether they liked it or not…

Ah, Borneo! That same Borneo that was once again on the menu in 1996, for a re-run of living hell in what would go down as one of toughest Camel Trophies ever. With barely 20 miles covered in ten days, this was hardcore stuff, and the Discoverys were put to the sternest of tests. The 4250-tonne (4183-ton) Superwinch, the snorkel, the cables to deflect tree branches, the full roll-cage, the Terratrip tripmeter and the satellite-navigation: it all came in useful in the struggle to hack through a habitat that frankly wasn't minded to let anyone past. You can only have nothing but praise for what were as near as anything production-spec 4x4s.

The vehicles were as much the stars as the contestants, and for good reason: with four people on board, a heavy load of equipment, and driving conditions that were challenging to say the least, and which had to tackled without flinching, the 4x4s of the Camel Trophy were truly all-action heroes.

▲ *You have to always be careful not to spend too long thinking about things…but also not to charge in head-down. Mistakes tend not to be pardoned. Lose concentration and you could have your Landie on its roof…*

▲ *Exhaustion, heat…and now the mud! This appalling bog demanded that everyone roll up their sleeves. Teams helping each other was the whole thing, during this episode in Guyana in 1992.*

◀ *Yves Truelle, one of the French team on the 1996 event in Borneo, had his work cut out: with a maximum of two to three hours of sleep a night, morale wasn't going to be hugely high, and he had to cope not just with mud but also with water…*

▼ *Borneo again, but this time in 1993. When the obstacles were serious and to boot had to be surmounted at night, there was no scope for error. Often, the winches had to be called upon.*

▼ *In spite of the difficulties, the Discovery generally managed to find a way through. This was sometimes with a bit of a hand from the experts.*

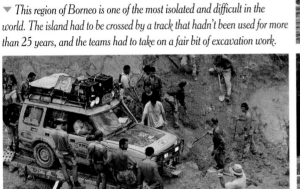

▼ *This region of Borneo is one of the most isolated and difficult in the world. The island had to be crossed by a track that hadn't been used for more than 25 years, and the teams had to take on a fair bit of excavation work.*

▲ *French team member Denis Rozand takes the lead in the convoy, as the Discoverys are winched through a marsh section.*

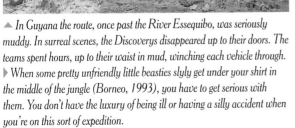

▲ *In Guyana the route, once past the River Essequibo, was seriously muddy. In surreal scenes, the Discoverys disappeared up to their doors. The teams spent hours, up to their waist in mud, winching each vehicle through.*
▶ *When some pretty unfriendly little beasties slyly get under your shirt in the middle of the jungle (Borneo, 1993), you have to get serious with them. You don't have the luxury of being ill or having a silly accident when you're on this sort of expedition.*

▲▲▲▲▲ *Once out of the Guatemalan jungle, it was necessary to get to the other river bank. As the pictures show, nothing is harder than crossing a river in a 4x4 if you don't have the necessary skills. And apparently not all the teams did…*

▼ *With its long-travel coil-sprung beam axles, the Discoverys could tackle the Chilean mountains without any worries; equipment included an electric Superwinch and extra lights.*

▼▼▼▼▼ *Mongolia isn't as flat as you might think, and hides some treacherous inclines. That year the Land Rovers had a roof-rack to carry a kayak: one guesses the boat didn't survive this impressive roll…*

The three principal French-organised rallies run in conjunction with big competitive endurance 'raids' are those that are partnered with the Optic 2000 Tunisie, Orpi Maroc and Master Rallye events. You can enjoy breathtaking scenery that the competitors don't have time to appreciate, and benefit from their facilities.

Rallies for all tastes

The 4x4 is the perfect tool for making an adventure out of your motoring. Who is there who hasn't dreamt of chucking it all in and leaving at the wheel of his – or her – favourite machine for a world of constantly changing scenery, without any worries about time or money? Well, that might be a bit extreme, because we all have our family commitments, our money restraints, and so on. But there are solutions, ways in which you can get away from it all with a like-minded bunch of people, and have a bundle of fun in the process.

The 4x4 magazines are always advertising rallies in all parts of the world, of varying difficulty and with a varying emphasis on competition and more tourist-inclined activities. Some are so popular that just having been able to participate is a bit like having a trophy on the wall! There's something of that in say the Malaysian Rainforest Challenge or the Togo Trophy, for example.

At the other extreme are those milder events that are more tailored to less specialist vehicles. Sometimes the two come together, with the organisers of some 4x4 endurance rallies organising a parallel event for less dedicated enthusiasts, making use of the same basic route and sometimes sharing facilities with the main event. You can benefit from the high-level organisation, and at the same time see rather more of the countryside than those who are locked horn-to-horn in the rally proper.

The Croisière Blanche is perhaps the best-known and most popular 'raid' in France. It takes place at the beginning of January and is based around the Orcières-Merlette ski-station in the Haute-Provence Alps – four days of the white powder, but also some good old mudplugging in the valleys! Yes, chains are a good idea…

The Raid Bleu takes place in Beaujolais country, around the pleasant commune of Régné-Durette, famous for the wine of that name. As with the Croisière Blanche, you can be part of the mudlark contingent of 'raiders', or you can take gang-planked alternative routes over some of the more difficult stages. And it goes without saying that food and wine play a certain part in the event!

▶ The Rainforest Challenge is reckoned to be the most difficult 'raid' on the planet. Over ten days and 1000 miles, contestants have to do battle with the jungles of the Malayan peninsula – in full monsoon season to boot.

▼ They're off – again! Goodbye Camel Trophy and hello G4 Challenge, a 4000-mile trial with four legs: New York to Quebec, South Africa, Australia, and finally a return to Utah. It is open to 16 countries, but with only one candidate per country allowed, selected from the numerous applicants lured by the Challenge's free entry. All types of Land Rover are used, and as with the Camel Trophy a multitude of open-air sports are included in the programme.

◀ The Jeep Jamboree is one of the oldest-established and best-known rallies, and is reserved – as you might expect – for Jeeps. You get the chance to see the most extraordinary variety of different models, in a superb setting.

▲ ▼ Yes, I know some of you will laugh, as the Trophée des Gazelles is more competition than rally, and it's only open to ladies. The idea, over seven days, is to find markers hidden in the countryside, with only a compass, a map, the car's standard mileometer, and your own good judgement – no sat-nav allowed. Needless to say the ever-changing contours of the Moroccan landscape don't help much, either. It's a tougher event than you'd think, and now has a well-deserved mixed equivalent, the 1000 Kasbahs rally.

▲ ▼ A French former winner of the Camel Trophy, Denis Rozand has set up a team to take people into deepest Togo. Depending on who is involved, the event can be either accessible to anyone or a re-run of the Camel Trophy. The VW Iltis 4x4s are provided.

The oddballs: production vehicles

▲ *Whatever was Pontiac thinking of, when it came up with the Aztek? With its gormless looks – and that colour! – they would have done better to have kept it in a darkened room. Both 2wd and 4wd versions are available; sales, unsurprisingly, aren't up to much.*

▲ ▼ ▶ *This is the 4x4 that is trying to be a sports-prototype. The BMW X5 Le Mans is a little bit of fun from BMW, and has remained a one-off. How about a 700bhp V12, a 5 seconds 0–60mph time, maximum speed close to 175mph, and roadholding to match?*

Across the world you're always going to have the exceptions, the freaks. Maybe they'll be made in relatively large numbers, maybe they'll be made just as a handful of bespoke machines for the very rich; maybe they'll simply remain one-offs. Some will be simple devices, some will be elaborate high-tech showcases based on a production vehicle.

Then there's the kit car scene in the UK and the States. It's cottoned onto the fact that 4x4s built on a chassis make the ideal basis for a kit car. In Britain this has led to devices such as the Dakar, while in the US you can make your own Hummer replica, using an old Ford pick-up and a kit supplied by the wonderfully-named Urban Gorilla company.

Remember, too, that every idea has its moment. It might have seemed pretty strange for Lamborghini to make a massive V12-powered 4x4, back in the 1980s, but now the Rambo Lambo seems almost normal, given that even Porsche has ventured into the off-road market, with its Cayenne. And what about the twin-engined Citroën 2CV? We've yet to see a twin-engined production car – or have we? Hybrid cars such as the Toyota Prius are now a reality, and this has led to a hybrid Lexus 4x4 with a petrol engine assisted by an electric motor – the first hybrid off-roader.

With the 4x4 movement showing no signs of waning, we are going to see plenty more oddball four-wheel-drivers in the future.

▲ ▶ *Méga is a French firm that makes Méhari-like leisure vehicles. But the boss, Georges Blain, is a true car nut, and he came up with the Méga Track, a cross between a Dakar-style buggy and a sports-GT. ◀ The interior is suitably luxurious, and back in 1995 it already boasted a video camera instead of a rear-view mirror. The intended clientele was rich arabs in the emirates who wanted to go sand-racing. The engine was a Mercedes 6.0 V12 delivering 395bhp, there was adjustable air suspension, and permanent 4wd with a locking rear diff. In all 17 were sold, with a price tag in the region of £190,000.*

▼ Mr Pachiaudi is well known in the off-road world, having won the Rallye des Cimes seven times and been French off-road champion 13 times. He's been making buggies for many years and the latest evolution of his excrutiatingly-named Bugey Bug has 4wd and a 115bhp Renault 2.1-litre turbo-diesel.

▲ The twin-engined Mini-Moke of 1962–63 was the brainchild of Alec Issigonis. Three prototypes were built – the first having linked clutch and throttle controls but separate gearlevers for each engine. The subsequent cars had the two gearlevers linked, as here.

▼ The 'Twini-Moke' project led to a single-engined small 4x4 based on BMC 1100 parts. Called the Austin Ant, it came close to production.

◀▶ Only 3500 of the Mitsubishi Pajero Evolution were made, all in right-hand drive. Just as with the WRC specials such as the Lancer Evo, its manufacture allowed the Japanese marque to homologate the basic design as a starting point for the Pajero T2, winner of the 1998 Dakar.

◀▼ A magical V12 engine in a Lamborghini 4x4: the end-of-the-'80s LM 02 was barking! It really was a forerunner of current trends, and even almost 20 years after its launch at the 1986 Turin show it still cuts it as an off-roader. The 5.2-litre V12 punted out 450bhp, and there was permanent 4x4, a low-ratio gearbox, and all-independent suspension.

◀ The Dakar kit is a neat way of rescuing a corroded Range Rover – and creating an even better off-roader in the process, as it's much lighter; Dakars can also be based on the Discovery I.

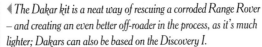

◀ The Citroën 2CV 4x4 (briefly known as the Sahara) was intended for oil-industry use in the North African desert. Its peculiarity was that 4wd was achieved by having two engines, the second 425cc unit being in the boot. Power was 24bhp – or 28bhp in later versions, and the car was claimed to be able to climb a 40% gradient and to have a maximum speed on tarmac of 60mph. In all 694 were made, between 1960 and 1966.

▶ *This tracked Land Rover was the work of Scottish firm Cuthbertson.*

▲ *Rod Millen is a Toyota nut, and well-known Toyota driver, in the States, and he has come up with this very special BJ lookalike. Underneath that sexy bodywork is the chassis and running gear of the big US-built 4.7-litre V8 Toyota Tundra pick-up.*

▲ *Meanwhile down in Corsica Francis Kosciolek has come up with his take on the American big-wheel 'rockcrawlers', with this self-built Nissan Patrol.*

Oddball machines: the privateers

When it's a private enthusiast doing his own thing, the sky's the limit. In the old days, modifications were mild and often geared to something as eminently sensible as improving the fuel consumption of the Range Rover by fitting a Nissan diesel. Alternatively, there was a fad in the late 1970s and early 1980s for custom Range Rovers, lavishly trimmed and perhaps with an extended wheelbase, maybe with six wheels, or else with convertible coachwork.

But with off-roading becoming ever more popular, the building of 'specials' has taken off. What begun with a few guys putting V8s in ex-Army Lightweight Land Rovers has developed into a vibrant custom scene, with devices such as cut-down shorter-wheelbase Range Rovers fighting it out in Euro trials with modified Jeeps or Japanese vehicles.

The Americans do it bigger and better, of course – but then they have the terrain to match. In the States the name of the game is 'rock-crawling', which is just what is sounds, with the 4x4s having quite literally to climb up rocks. This has led to a breed of jacked-up off-roaders, with extended spring mountings, special long-travel suspension systems, and bodies lifted higher off their chassis. 'Lift kits' offer anything from 2½in to 12in jack-ups – and the resultant axle articulation can be mind-boggling. Helping the process along, special I-beam suspension arms are available for some models, transforming the front suspension into a massive twin swing-arm set-up.

Then there's up-engining, and the Americans aren't afraid of making a little Suzuki into a real fire-breather by fitting a Detroit V6 or V8.

◀▲ *Mohammed Ben Sulayem is the organiser of the UAE Desert Challenge in Dubai and the boss of a superbly equipped garage where he concocted this wild Toyota.*

▶ *More than 600bhp has been extracted from the 4.5-litre straight-six, thanks to twin turbochargers. It is so powerful that you get wheelspin at all four wheels in third gear!*

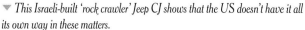

▼ *This Israeli-built 'rock crawler' Jeep CJ shows that the US doesn't have it all its own way in these matters.*

▲▲▼ *The maddest of the Big Foot brigade! 'Gravedigger' is the US champ in this category, with a little help from a blown 9.5-litre V8 belting out 1600bhp on methanol. It is nearly 12ft high, has wheels that weigh 5cwt, wheel travel that's measured in yards, and fuel range in minutes – ten minutes a tankload, if you're counting.*

▼ *Russia's answer to the Hummer? The Caïman was created by a rich St Petersburg businessman, as a shop-window for his company. All it needs is a decent engine, as its Lada four-pot isn't really up to shifting more than 3 tons of heavy metal.*

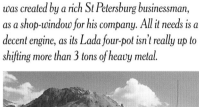

▲ *Back on Planet Sensible, this Auverland has been developed for off-road trials, and benefits from light weight, long suspension travel, and separate right-hand and left-hand braking.*

▼ *The Grand Cherokee isn't often chosen by customisers, who tend to go more for the CJ7 or the Wrangler. But this lift-kitted 'crawler' does look the business…*

◀▲▼ *Another high-camp offering from the film industry, this Land Rover was specially kitted-out for action heroine Lara Croft. All this for two minutes of screen time…*

▼ *Mercedes ML, Light Tank model. Well, not quite, but this horror was dreamt up for the Jurassic Park sequel, to replace the Ford Explorer used in the first film.*

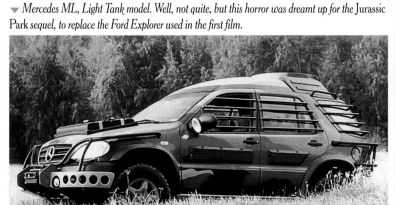

The many faces of off-roading

▶ *The Toyota RAV4, which made its appearance in 1993 in Japan and in 1995 in Europe, marked the arrival of a new breed of 4x4s more orientated towards road use.*

▲▼ *The RAV4 was soon sufficiently successful to spawn a four-door version, with the same lively 128bhp 16-valve 2-litre petrol engine.*

▲▼ *Honda was hot on Toyota's heels with the CRV. Launched at the 1995 Tokyo show, it was soon a big hit, not least because of its generous internal space.*

Tarmac warriors

With Toyota's RAV4 a new breed of 4x4 made its appearance: an SUV for those people who weren't likely to get their tyres muddy but who appreciated the feeling of security given by a chunky off-roader. Toyota's master-stroke was to combine tough-guy looks (exposed spare wheel and all) with handling and roadholding that was on a par with that of a decent hot-hatch. The pay-off was mud-plugging abilities a good few notches below something such as a Land Rover – but which were still good enough to help you out of trouble if the going got a bit sticky.

With this new class of 4x4 out goes any idea of having a transfer box or even, in many instances, a lockable centre diff, even if such a device is pretty handy in slippery conditions. Instead, various new types of transmission have been developed, with viscous couplings or other forms of electrically-activated coupling bringing four-wheel drive into operation as soon as a loss of traction is detected. In normal use, on tarmac, only one pair of wheels is driven (the front, on the Honda CRV or the Nissan X-Trail, for example), but when needed, drive can be distributed to the other axle, up to 100 per cent. If the first such systems were somewhat unsophisticated, they have now given way to highly-evolved electronically-controlled set-ups with individual traction control at each wheel – an arrangement that is so effective that it has now started to be found on a good number of real off-roaders. Meanwhile the smaller SUVs have been joined by bigger sisters, such as the Lexus RX300.

▲ *Long-time market leader in the small 4x4 class, Suzuki joined the SUV party with its Grand Vitara. But it came with a trick up its sleeve: a high-low transfer box which was pretty much unique in the class.*

◀ *Land Rover joined the fray with its Freelander, announced at the 1997 Frankfurt show. It went on to become the European market leader in its sector, thanks in good part to the availability of a turbo-diesel.*

▼ *The SUV market has attracted plenty of manufacturers, but Renault was the first to combine 4wd with a midi-MPV, with its Scénic RX4; the four-wheel-drive system distributes power to the rear wheels when it senses the front wheels starting to slip.*

◀ *Mitsubishi unveiled its Pinin in 1999; it is available either with full-time 4wd (and a viscous coupling and centre diff) or with selectable 4wd (with low-range gearing and lockable centre diff). The top engine is a 130bhp direct-injection 2.0-litre petrol unit.*

▲ *The Subaru Forester can't really be classed as an SUV – consider it more as an estate that happens to have 4wd. But with its transfer box and its torquey flat-four engine, it's nobody's patsy if the going gets rough – especially in 177bhp turbocharged form.*

▲ *The X-Trail interior is crisply and originally styled, with a central instrument binnacle, a large sunroof, and refrigerated cubbies for drinks cans.*

▲ *The Hyundai Santa Fe is Korea's first crossover SUV, and has plenty in its favour, not least the peppy diesel engine found in the CRTD GSI version.*

▲ *Top-of-range Freelander, Santa Fe and Grand Vitara models all offer V6 petrol engines with a useful degree of poke.*

▲ *The Honda CRV has – inevitably – become bigger in its second-generation form, the wheelbase increasing by 3½in. Power is up, too, to 150bhp.*

▲ *Nissan was a tail-end Charlie in coming to the SUV market, with its X-Trail – but the wait was worth it. Only available as a five-door, the X-Trail has either a 114bhp direct-injection 2.2-litre diesel or a 140bhp petrol 2-litre.*

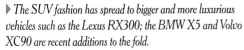

▲ *The second-generation RAV4 arrived in 2000 – bigger, sleeker, and also available in some markets with only two-wheel drive. For the first time, too, a turbo-diesel was on offer.*

▶ *The SUV fashion has spread to bigger and more luxurious vehicles such as the Lexus RX300; the BMW X5 and Volvo XC90 are recent additions to the fold.*

How they were: the best-sellers as they were 20-odd years ago. From left to right are the 1979 Mitsubishi L200, the 1979 Toyota Hilux, and the King Cab version of the 1980 Nissan pick-up.

The 4x4 pick-up: metamorphosis for a workhorse

In 1982 the L200 gained a 2.5-litre diesel engine (other engines were 2-litre and 2.6-litre petrol and 2.3-litre diesel); the style was a generation behind that of the saloon cars.

The 4x4 version of the Hilux sat noticeably higher, on larger tyres. The interior was well equipped, and wouldn't have shamed a car.

By the late 1980s all three makes had discovered the double cab, a configuration that together with 4wd created an ideal work-cum-play leisure vehicle. This is a 1987 Nissan double-cab model.
By 1992 Mitsubishi was offering a strong contender in the class with its revised L200. With smart wheels, bullbar and duo-tone paint, it was a long way removed from a small-town builder's workhorse.

The pick-up has been around since the dawn of motoring, but before the Second World War it was pretty much an American phenomenon – although the French did have their wood-backed *camionnette normande* and their tailgated *torpédo commerciale* derivatives of open touring cars. The first car-based British pick-up was the Bedford 6wt Utility Wagon of 1939.

All this changed with the war, when most UK manufacturers developed car-derived pick-ups for the forces. Called light utilities, or 'tillies' for short, they led most makers to produce pick-up variants of their post-war cars.

Up until the mid-1950s a large proportion of these went to Australia, another country that played an important part in the development of the pick-up: back in 1933 it was Ford of Australia that created the 'Coupé Utilty', Australia's first closed-cab car-derived pick-up. Holden followed, with 'utes' based on Chevrolets, Buicks and Willys, and the body style became a national institution.

But the European pick-up began to fade out in the 1970s, the last players – until Skoda's Favorit came along – being the Sierra-based Ford P100 and Peugeot's 504 pick-up. It was left to the Japanese to corral the market, and they were thus sitting happy when the pick-up came back into favour, as a leisure vehicle, preferably with four-wheel drive.

Responding to this US-led trend, the end of the 1970s and the beginning of the 1980s had already seen the first 4wd Japanese 'half-ton' pick-ups, in the shape of the Mitsubishi Forte L200, the 4wd Toyota Hilux, and the Nissan King Cab 4x4. Intended primarily for the US, these vehicles, and those offered by Isuzu and Mazda, were soon finding a ready market in Europe, on account of their manageable size. Since then they have become better equipped, and with the spread of double-cab four-door versions they have become an important part of the 4wd market.

▲ *Nissan responded with softer lines for its pick-up range, and similarly glitzy presentation options. The double-cab here is pure USA in its look – down to the side steps and the chrome roll bar.*

◄ *The Toyota Hilux kept the same basic lines from 1989 until 2002. The 2.5-litre diesel gave way to a 2.3-litre turbo-diesel, subsequently up-gunned to 2.5 litres.*

◄ *The Isuzu pick-up is better known in Britain as Vauxhall Brava; production in this form ended in 2003, and a replacement is not immediately likely.*

▲ *The latest Hilux has softer lines, and now has a common-rail direct-injection diesel in either 88bhp or intercooled 102bhp form; again the double cab is only available as a 4x4.*

▲ *Mazda's equivalent in what used to be known as the 'half-ton' pick-up class is today the B-2500. Standard-cab, extended-cab and double-cab formats are available.*

◄▲ *The L200 has stiff competition these days. The current version, launched in 2001, now has a variable-geometry turbo which pushes power up to 115bhp.*

▼ *Nissan's Navara 4x4 is its top-of-range 4x4 pick-up, available as a King Cab or a double-cab; a 2wd version is not available, at least in the UK.*

▲▼ *Nissan's Navara is now a smart well-styled vehicle, and with power of 133bhp it is quite a nifty mover too. The chrome grille is standard, as are 16in alloy wheels.*

◄ *The Ford Ranger is built in the same factories as the Mazda.*

No – not a refugee encampment in the Balkans. This is the Val d'Isère 4x4 show, which in terms of the area covered is the biggest in the world. Part of the event is held in the valley of the famous ski resort, and the rest higher up, at an altitude of 8000–9000ft, in the Espace Killy ski-station. The off-road tracks are unbelievable, and all the manufacturers are on hand to demonstrate their wares. A memorable if sometimes hair-raising experience for visitors…

Off-road shows: visit and be amazed

▲ *Yes, a field full of Nissans. Hats off, though, to the Japanese firm, for setting up the Nissan Adventure Club to organise events in France and abroad for owners of its 4x4s.*

With something over a hundred Land-Rover clubs in Britain – not to mention other off-road clubs – there are always going to be things going on at the weekend to attract the 4x4 enthusiast who wants a break from trialling.

Top show, though, has to be 'Billing', the Land Rover Enthusiast Show, to give the event its full name, held at Billing Aquadrome in Northamptonshire. Established in 1991 and today sponsored by *Land Rover Enthusiast* magazine, it claims to be the biggest family Land Rover event in the world – which is a bit of a downer, of course, if you're into Jeeps. That apart, there's something for everyone, with an off-road course, Land Rover factory folk demonstrating their wares, a strong military element, and more Landie specialists than you could shake a broken halfshaft at: not to be missed!

And what goes for Britain goes for other countries. You can also be sure to find something to tickle your fancy – or shock the socks off you – at some of the more extravagant trade shows and motor shows around the world. The US motor shows, in particularly the Detroit Motor Show, are always a good place to catch the latest off-the-wall concept cars, while the SEMA show in Las Vegas – SEMA is short for Speciality Equipment Marketing Association – is a trade-only showcase for the automotive after-market…which means that every wild add-on and bit of tuning and modification kit on the market is likely to be on view. That means some pretty extraordinary 4x4s on display, amongst other things.

But if you're more into participation than gawping, how about a 4x4 training course or a couple of days in an agreeable country hotel as part of a weekend of expert off-road instruction? This is something the British do very well, and there are some long-established specialists – look in the magazines to find out more. As a way of having a break and coming back having learnt something, it must be hard to beat…

▲ ▼ *It's a family thing, the 4x4 world. Miniature Jeeps and Land Rovers are the perfect way of getting junior hooked, and the big shows will have reduced-scale off-roaders for sale. Dads lock up your wallets…*

▲ *Mercedes has its own club in some countries – sometimes supported by the company, even if the club is an independent entity.*

▼ *Companies such as Land Rover are keen supporters of the major events, so you can count on knowledgeable advice from the guys who made the car in the first place. Failing that, 101 independent experts will be on hand…*

◀ *If you want to hone your skills – or maybe just learn for the first time how to drive off-road, then there are countless courses around the country to which you can sign up.*

▲ *In some countries you'll find clubs for less common vehicles: here is a gathering of the French-based Toyota Land Cruiser Association.*

▲ *The Land Rover event at Billing each summer is the biggest gathering for Land Rover enthusiasts from around the world, and features off-road demonstrations, arena events and a huge selection of clubs and specialists. Closest to camera in this shot is another of those Belgian-assembled Minerva Land Rovers.*

▲ ◀ ▶ *The big motor shows are the place to catch the latest 4x4 concept cars – and to do a bit of comparison window-shopping. You might even bump into the charming ladies fron Nissan Racing…*

◀ ▲ ▼ ▶ *The SEMA show in Las Vegas is the big US car-accessory trade jamboree. But it's not all battery-charger wholesalers: there's some wild 4x4 stuff on which you can feast your eyes.*

In the States, 4 Wheel Drive and Sport Utility Magazine majors on the vehicles used in rock-crawling events, and has a strong technical flavour.

Much the same can be said of its rival, Off Road, which plugs 'Form. Function. Attitude'.

The two best-selling British Land Rover magazines are market-leader Land-Rover Owner International and Land Rover Enthusiast, the latter edited by Rover historian James Taylor.

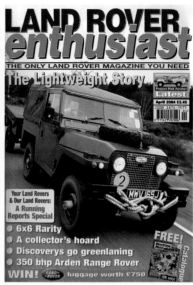

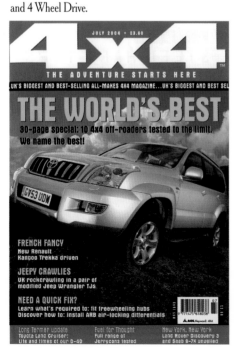

The major British off-road magazine is EMAP's 4x4, which can trace its origins back to the 1980s merger of 4 Wheel Drive and Overlander to form Off-Road and 4 Wheel Drive.

Read all about it!

The specialist press has become more specialist – that's one of the self-evident truths of the past decade or so. This applies to the off-road world as much as any other sector of the motoring market. If the UK can support two national Mini magazines, for example, then it's no great surprise that there are now four Land-Rover magazines on the shelves, and a couple of general off-road magazines.

The US has its share of magazines, as you'd expect, and they occupy particular niches – although it's probably true to say that trail-driving, rockcrawling and the construction of high-riding rockcrawler specials feature more strongly than other genres of off-roading. Beyond this, pick-ups and 'soft-road' SUVs are more the thing, whether 4wd or not.

In Australia the flavour is very different. The country's top-seller, *Australian 4wd Monthly*, has a firm emphasis on travelling in the bush and outback, and its advertisements include fair numbers for camping trailers, small generators and the all-important fridges for keeping tinnies of the amber nectar suitably cool. South Africa's *Leisure Wheels* has a similar exploration-biased content, and generally has features on trails and safaris in South Africa and surrounding countries.

Japan's chunky 4x4 Magazine isn't one for the dirty digits brigade: you're more likely to find a comparison of glovebox sizes than a guide about how to jack up your Land Cruiser. In any case, it's all in Japanese…

The Japanese, meanwhile, do things in their usual large-scale beautifully-produced way. The layout and content might be challenging to any western enthusiast who flicks through the doorstep-sized *4x4 Magazine*, all 256 glossy pages of it, but the quality feel is unrivalled. There's no grubby-finger stuff, and lots of picture-gallery reportage of current up-market SUVs, but turn to the back (which is the front, if you follow, in a Japanese magazine), and you'll see from the events reports that rockcrawling has a strong Japanese enthusiast base, with lift-kitted Suzukis quite common and a sprinkling of Mitsubishi-badged Jeeps joining the fray.

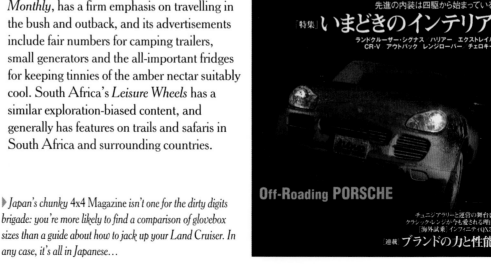

▶ *Along with Auto Verde, the Spanish magazine 4x4 Solo Auto covers the off-road market in Spain.*

▶ *Leading French magazine L'Auto-Journal has now added a 4x4 title to its stable. Detailed tests and hard-nosed journalism are on the menu.*

▼ *Britain's 4x4 Mart covers new vehicles, road tests and club and show listings, and has a strong Land Rover section.*

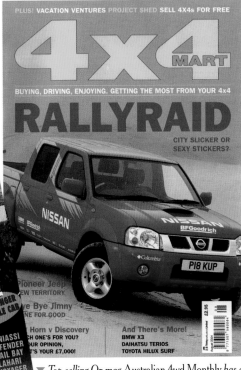

▲ *The French even have a magazine for the Toyota Land Cruiser – which is more than can be said for the British. The same publishing house also offers a magazine on Land Rovers.*
▶ *South Africa is prime 4x4 country, and Leisure Wheels locks into the world of veld-bashing, safaris and adventure off-roading in southern Africa.*

▼ *Top-selling Oz mag Australian 4wd Monthly has a good mix of editorial, and some fascinating reports on back-of-beyond trekking in the outback. The tone is typically laid-back Aussie…*

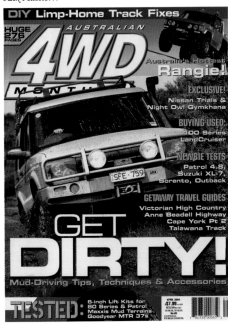

▲ *In France, 4x4 Magazine was the second off-road magazine to appear, and dates back to 1981. Unsurprisingly, reporting of raids in North Africa feature strongly, given France's attachment to what were once its colonies.*
▶ *Looking after German interests is Off Road, billed as 'The Magazine for Freedom on Wheels'. Can't say fairer than that, can you?*

The manufacturers

Jeep (Daimler-Chrysler)

▲▼ *The two most recent generations of Jeep Wrangler, the YJ (top) with its rectangular headlamps, and the TJ (below) with its more traditional round-headlamp front.*

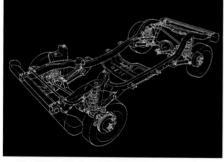

The last big novelty from Jeep appeared at the end of 2001: called the Jeep Liberty in the States, it was the replacement for the Cherokee, whose name it keeps in the European market. The Cherokee – which dated from 1983 – was the first genuinely modern Jeep and hardly changed much over the years, at least as far as its looks were concerned. So the '02 Cherokee is an important watershed in the history of the world's oldest 4x4 marque, which was beginning to look a bit old-fashioned in its styling. The new-look Cherokee is resolutely modern and turns its back on the square-cut lines of the 1980s – a harbinger of things to come when the new-generation Jeep range extends to encompass a new Wrangler any moment soon, to replace the current TJ launched in 1996.

The other big news for the marque is the beginning of a closer collaboration with Mercedes, now that Jeep is part of the Daimler-Chrysler group. The first fruit has been the arrival under the bonnet of the Grand Cherokee of the excellent Mercedes 2.7-litre turbo-diesel used in the M-class. It seems likely that Mecedes power units will eventually be used in all Jeeps, beginning with the diesels – where Europe is far ahead of the US in terms of technology. Meanwhile, the good old yankee V8 still has its place, not least in the top-of-range Grand Cherokees, such as the Overland model that was launched in 2002 as a tribute to the Jeep's original manufacturer, Willys-Overland of Toledo, Ohio. This luxury model with its 258bhp engine is a riposte to the growing competition from the likes of the BMW X5, Mercedes ML and Lexus RX300, which have become increasingly popular in the States.

▲ *The TJ, launched in 1996, brought with it coil-spring beam-axle front suspension and a coil-sprung live rear axle.*

▶ *Since 1992, when the Grand Cherokee came out, there has been a three-model range: Wrangler, Cherokee and Grand Cherokee.*

◀▲ *The Wrangler remains a symbol of four-wheeled America. It uses two petrol engines: a 2.5-litre 'four' (currently not UK-available) and a 174bhp 4-litre in-line 'six'; either a five-speed manual transmission or a three-speed automatic can be specified.*

▼▶ The Wrangler is available as a soft-top or with a full hard-top. The base SE model (not UK-available) is supplemented by Sport and top-of-range Sahara variants; specifications vary from market to market.

▼ The Grand Cherokee has been the first Jeep to benefit from the Chrysler-Mercedes marriage, having been given the M-series direct-injection in-line five-cylinder diesel, good for 161bhp at 4000rpm and maximum torque of 295lb ft at 1800rpm.

▼▼ The current Jeep Cherokee has forsaken angular lines for more curved forms. The front with its vertical bars and round headlamps provides a visual link with the TJ-series Wrangler.

▲ The new Cherokee has a modern and well-presented cockpit. There are three equipment levels, the top being the Limited.

◀▲▼ If the six-cylinder 4-litre has disappeared from the catalogues, the Grand Cherokee today deploys two 4701cc petrol V8s, of 224bhp (and 287lb ft of torque at 3750rpm) and 255bhp (and 309lb ft at 4000rpm); it is this last unit that is found in the Overland.

▲ The Grand Cherokee is more luxurious, fittingly enough, and has a higher level of equipment. It is only available with a four-speed or five-speed automatic transmission.

◀ The Cherokee is currently available with four engines: a 2.4-litre 145bhp petrol 'four', a four-pot 2.5-litre 141bhp diesel, a 2.8-litre 148bhp diesel, and a 3.7-litre petrol V6 developing 201bhp.

Land Rover: here's to the next 50 years!

The English marque has seen several owners these past few years, before ending up part of Ford. But – for the moment, at least – it has stayed a separate entity, with its own dedicated factory at Solihull. The range has been completely overhauled and has been going great guns since the 1997 arrival of the Freelander, which has been a huge success and has led to a doubling of worldwide sales.

Since then there has been the new third-generation Range Rover, designed when BMW owned the company. Bigger, more luxurious and more stuffed with technology than its predecessor, it has added to the marque's prestige. It has now been joined by a new 'MkIII' Discovery, the first Land Rover to be wholly developed under Ford.

To be called the LR3 in the States, this is a vastly important model for the marque, being an all-new design that is expected to be the company's biggest money-earner and having an architecture (monocoque-on-chassis 'Integrated Body-Frame') from which future generations of its sister models will be derived. More spacious, so that it is a genuine seven-seater, the third-generation 'Disco', launched in 2004, has all-independent suspension – by coils or air springs, depending on model – and is powered either by a 24-valve 2720cc V6 turbo-diesel delivering 190bhp or a 295bhp adaptation of the 4394cc 32-valve Jaguar V8.

Despite the Discovery's move up-market, there is still a gap between it and the king-sized Range Rover, and the next new product to see the light of day is expected to be a development of the Range Stormer concept car unveiled in early 2004 – in other words, a sportier and less bulky Range Rover with a lower roofline. As for the Range Rover itself, this will ultimately shed its BMW-sourced engines for power units from the Ford group.

▲ *The final versions of the Discovery II had a restyled front with the same overlapping-lamp look as the new Range Rover; gradually the 'Disco' has crept up-market.*

▲ *The new Discovery 3 – that's how Land Rover renders it – has simple unornamented lines that admirably communicate the marque's key value of rugged practicality.*

▲ *The 184bhp petrol 4-litre V8 on the Discovery II was accompanied by a 138bhp 2.5-litre Td5 which was very popular on the continent.*

▲ *The Range Stormer concept was unveiled in 2004: it's a looker, you have to admit! The production version won't be anything like as startling, and will have four normally-hinged doors.*

▲ *The tailgate is now a two-part horizontally-split unit, and the spare wheel has moved indoors. The wheelbase is 14in longer than that of the Discovery II.*
▶ *Launched in 1997, the Freelander is the most car-like and the least out-and-out off-road of the range; engines are transverse and suspension all-independent. Power comes from 1.8-litre 4-cylinder (120bhp) or 2-litre V6 (177bhp) K-series engines or a 112bhp turbo-diesel Td4 unit. A particular feature of the Freelander is its innovatory Hill Descent Control.*

◄ *Although not designed for the rough-and-tumble, the Freelander's off-road ability is more than competent; it is available either as a Soft-back three-door, with optional hardtop, or as a more conventional five-door.*

▲ *In spite of its high price and its luxury image, there's no reason why a Range Rover can't leave the tarmac and prove its still impressive off-road credentials.*

▼ *The Range Rover uses two BMW-sourced power units: a 4.4-litre petrol V8 (285bhp and 325lb ft of torque at 3600rpm) and a 3-litre straight-six Td6 turbo-diesel (177bhp and 287lb ft of torque at 2000rpm); expect Ford/Jaguar engines in the future…*

▲ *The Defender, king of the muddy-tyre brigade, seems to have plenty of life in front of it. Replacing it will be some challenge.*

▶ *The Defender remains available in three wheelbases – 90in, 110in and 130in – and even the longest is no dunce off-road.*

▼ *Thanks to its spaciousness, its modernity and its lavish equipment, the Range Rover is virtually without a rival in Europe. It's not been doing too badly for itself in the US, either, it's good to be able to report.*

▲ *The three-door Freelander interior has a different configuration from that of the five-door: there are individual rear seats with a tray between them.*

▼ *Even in its more basic version, without the pale wood detailing, the cockpit of the Range Rover isn't missing any gear. The suspension uses adjustable air springs, and there's permanent 4wd, a Torsen centre diff, traction control, and Hill Descent Control.*

▲ *The Defender has now been reduced to just the Td5 engine, with the disappearance of the old Rover V8.*

▼ *From whatever angle you look at it, the Range Rover is undeniably a styling success.*

▲ *The G-Class was conceived in collaboration with Steyr-Daimler-Puch. In Austria, Switzerland and the former Comecon countries the 'G' carried Puch badging until a few years ago.*

▲▲▼ *Early cockpits were pretty rudimentary, reflecting the utility/military uses to which many G-Classes would be put. The design team was largely drawn from Hanomag-Henschel, the light-truck manufacturer which M-B had acquired a few years previously. By the driver's seat are the levers for the two diff locks, with the low-high and 2wd/4wd selector behind. Later G-Classes have permanent four-wheel drive.*

▲ *Three body styles are offered: swb station wagon, swb soft-top, and lwb station wagon. Vans in both wheelbases have also been available, along with a lwb five-door soft-top for military use.*

Mercedes – shining star of 4x4s

Mercedes came to the 4x4 scene relatively late, but its G-Class, assembled at the Steyr works in Graz, Austria, is a typically thorough piece of design, built around robust truck-derived components. Launched in 1979 and still very much in production, the G-Class is an intriguing hybrid: utilitarian and austerely-styled, it is at the same time more luxurious and better-suspended than a workhorse pure-and-simple in the Land Rover mould. By spring 2004 roughly 175,000 G-Classes had been made, and since it went on sale in the US at the end of 2001 demand has risen sharply.

Designed with more than half an eye to military use, the G-Class has served in various armies around the world, and it's a little-known fact that a run of G-Classes was assembled by Peugeot in France, with the Peugeot badge and Peugeot diesel engines, for use in the French army. The G-Class has also been assembled in Greece

Built on a separate chassis and having rigid coil-sprung axles front and rear, the 'G' has had permanent 4wd since 1990, in conjunction with front and rear diff locks and a fully-locking centre diff; a package of electronic stability/traction controls was added in 2001. A V8 joined the range in 1993, and in 1997 the Mercedes V6 replaced the in-line six-cylinder engine that until then had been the petrol mainstay. 2004 has seen the arrival of 'King G', the latest G55 AMG with its supercharged 5.4-litre V8. With 476bhp and a claimed 0–60mph time of 5.6 seconds, it's ample proof there's life yet in the old dog!

All the same, it's on the M-Class that Mercedes depends for serious volume. Built since 1997 in the M-B factory in Tuscaloosa, Alabama, the 'M' is aimed squarely at the leisure SUV market – although with its reduction gearbox and ABS-linked electronic torque distribution it is no sunny-days-only off-roader. All-independent suspension and a monocoque body indicate the principal vocation of the M-Class, however, as does its luxurious interior trim.

◀▲ *In 1989 the 'G' went over to permanent 4wd, and in order to face up to the more luxurious Range Rover gained an interior more in line with that of Mercedes saloons. Selectable ABS and electric diff locks were other new features, while for 1992 a new 3.5-litre turbo-diesel arrived and the 2.5-litre diesel gave way to a 2.9-litre unit. In 1994 it was the turn of the '300' to be up-gunned, and in came a 210bhp G320.*

▲ *The other feature of the ML is its twin-turbo V8 diesel, in the ML 400 CDI; kicking out 250bhp, at its launch it was the most powerful diesel on the market. Most European sales, however, have been of the lesser CDI.*

◀ ▲ ▶ *At the end of 1997 Mercedes unveiled the M-Class, at the Frankfurt show. More leisure-orientated than the 'G', it was also more modern in its styling and its technology, having all-independent suspension and permanent 4wd controlled electronically by an anti-slip mechanism. Optional was a third row of seats that folded sideways.*

▼ ▶ *To counter the BMW X5 the M-Class underwent quite a few changes at the end of 2001, gaining better finish and better equipment (sat-nav, sequential gearbox, individualised automatic air-con, and up to eight airbags), and a restructured model range of currently ML 350, ML 500 and ML 270 CDI in the UK.*

▲ ▼ ▼ *The ML 55 AMG is another kettle of fish: not only does it have a 347bhp V8, but it also boasts special interior trim, while outside there are long-range lamps set into the front bumper and a pair of serious-looking exhausts.*

◀ ▼ *The 'G' meanwhile, has continued to move up the luxury tree, while its engines are now shared with the M-Class. Standard are ESP ('Electronic Stability Program'), Brake Assist, and the 4ETS Electronic Traction System.*

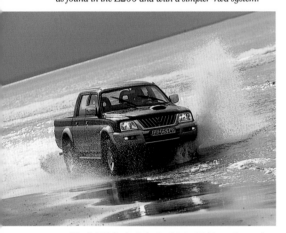

In the UK the entry-level Shogun is the 3.2-litre turbo-diesel, but in France, where the Shogun is sold as the Pajero, there is a 2.5 TD model with the same engine as found in the L200 and with a simpler 4wd system.

The L200 had a light facelift for 2002, and gained a variable-geometry turbo installation – good for 115bhp.

The L200 is a pick-up that's become civilised, and the latest-generation models are pretty much car-like inside, with electric windows, air-con, double airbags – and power steering, of course…

The double cab has a 5ft pick-up bed, against 7ft 4in for the single-cab model; load capacity of the 4 Life model is nearly 20cwt.
The third row of seats on lwb Shoguns folds flat into the floor, a neat arrangement.

Mitsubishi:
the triple-diamond marque

They're still at it, starring all over the world, and in particular in competition, where they have the record for the greatest number of victories in the Paris–Dakar. No doubt about it: the Shogun is the cornerstone of Mitsubishi's reputation, as well as the vehicle that has done more than most to popularise the 4x4.

Now in its third generation, the current Shogun bristles with state-of-the-art engineering: a monocoque shell, all-independent suspension, Super Select electronic-transfer 4wd, a computer-controlled five-speed INVECS II automatic gearbox with sequential Sports Mode shifting, and a limited-slip rear diff and central viscous coupling. With its high-low transfer box and locking central diff, plus Traction Control and Engine Brake Assist Control, it has all the kit for serious off-roading. As for the engine, the 3.5-litre twin-cam V6 has direct injection and four valves per cylinder, a recipe delivering 200bhp at 5000rpm. No need to apologise

for the diesel, either: a direct-injection 'four', the 3.2 TD DI-D is a twin-cam 16-valver and pushes out 160bhp at 3800rpm and 275lb ft of torque at 2000rpm, this without common-rail technology.

Backing up the Shogun are three supplementary models, the small Italian-built Shogun Pinin, with single-cam 1.8-litre or direct-injection 2.0-litre twin-cam petrol engines, the more sporting low-roof Shogun Sport, and the new Outlander crossover SUV-estate. This last uses a 2.4-litre four-cylinder petrol engine mated to an automatic gearbox, and has permanent 4wd. The marque's reputation also owes much to the L200 pick-up. One of the first leisure-orientated pick-ups, it is pretty much a reference vehicle in its class, and sales have soared in the UK, aided by a tax loophole. Most are four-wheel-drive (with 4wd selectable, and an electric diff lock), with the fully-specced double-cab models being the most popular.

Even in long-wheelbase form the Shogun is a real off-roader. It's also just as much at home on the motorway, especially with the long-legged petrol V6. For economy, though, better go for the turbo-diesel 'four'.
The Shogun interior is a pretty luxurious place to be these days. Three trim levels are available, their names varying from country to country. No, the wood isn't real…

▲▼ *The short-chassis cars are inevitably more agile than the long-chassis models, and having manual transmission also helps; with the V6, offered in the UK only on lwb cars, only automatic transmission is available.*

▲ *This French-market car is a swb V6 – although only the GDI badge on the grille gives it away – and doubtless lives up to the Pajero name, which means 'wild cat' in Japanese.*

▼ *The Shogun Sport was principally created for the US market, where it is sold as the Montero Sport and where lower-cost versions have only 2wd. For the UK, engines are 2.5TD or 3.0 V6 petrol.*

▼ *The Montero interior is certainly less luxurious than that of the third-generation Shogun, but none the worse for that.*

▲ *The second-generation Shogun carries on in some countries, under the name Montero; suspension is by torsion bars at the front and by coils (with a live axle) at the rear, while the 4wd system is less elaborate and still has a lockable rear diff.*

◀ *Three-door and five-door Monteros are available, and the 115bhp 2.5-litre turbo-diesel is the only engine on offer. Attractive pricing makes the Montero a good buy – but it's not offered to the Brits.*

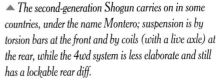

▲▼ *The Pinin is a smaller and more chic 4x4; unsurprisingly some of the advertising is aimed at the female market. The interior is simple and smart.*

▲ *The Pinin is available either with full-time 4wd (1.8 models) or with selectable 4wd (2.0 GDI); suspension is by strut at the front and by a coil-spring live back axle.*

▼ *The X-Trail has a monocoque body and all-independent suspension. The 'All-Mode' transmission automatically engages four-wheel drive when the slightest lack of traction is detected. In normal weather, on dry surfaces for example, the X-Trail functions as a front-wheel-drive vehicle.*

▲ *The X-Trail in the form shown at the 2000 Paris Motor Show. The roof locker with integral roof rails didn't make it to production. Equally, the show-car's interior (below) was toned down a bit.*

▲▲▼ *The inetrior of Nissan's midi-SUV has some original features, such as the large standard-fit sunroof, the central instruments, and the refrigerated bottle-holders. There are plenty of storage cubbies and the durably-covered loadspace includes a useful ski-hatch in the rear seat back.*

Nissan:
the Franco-Japanese axis

It might not have quite the aura of some of its rivals, but back in 2001 Nissan celebrated 50 years as a 4x4 maker – and the company goes back to 1911. Over the years the firm has gone though various evolutions, but the most important is the 1999 alliance with Renault, which has made the combined group the fourth-largest car manufacturer in the world. What does that mean for its four-wheel-drives? Almost certainly they will remain the domain of Nissan. Although in some markets the cars will carry the Renault badge, the design, development and manufacture will stay in Nissan's hands.

Meanwhile, that 4wd half-century has been celebrated with the 2001 model-year launch of the compact X-Trail, a well-received mid-sizer aimed at the Freelander sector. Unlike Toyota's RAV4, the X-Trail is only available as a five-door, and comes with 2-litre or 2.5-litre petrol engines or a 2.2-litre common-rail turbo-diesel; the lucky Japanese also have a 280bhp petrol turbo to light their fires.

The rest of the 4wd range comprises the pick-ups, the Terrano, and the famous Patrol that set the whole Nissan 4x4 ball rolling. The Terrano, made in Spain as a three-door and a five-door, continues to sell well (and is no longer made with Ford badges, as the Maverick), and comes with either 2.7-litre or direct-injection 3.0-litre turbo-diesel power; with its torsion-bar front and live coil-sprung rear, it is mechanically pretty conservative.

The same could be said, only more so, of the Patrol GR, which keeps coil-sprung rigid axles front and rear: but what you see is what you get with this brick-like 3-litre turbo-diesel: with its non-independent suspension, the Patrol is a superbly capable off-roader.

As for the pick-ups, these have now been smartened up, and have a chunky square-cut look inspired at least in part by US trends. Single-cab, king-cab and double-cab configurations are available, and the Nissans are firmly competitive with the other Japanese offerings.

▼ ▼ *The Patrol GR now has a less utilitarian interior – at least for European markets – and the range-topping automatic version makes an agreeable cruiser.*

▲ ▼ *The Navara pick-up is Nissan's serious bid for a bigger slice of Europe's recreational pick-up market; the company has been a strong global player in pick-ups for decades.*

▲ *The X-Trail has decent off-road ability, thanks to a three-mode 4wd system: 2wd, Auto with an electronic sensor to apportion drive front-to-rear, and Lock, finally, which gives a fixed 57/43 split front-to-rear.*

▲ ▶ *The Patrol GR, meanwhile, plugs on, with the 3-litre turbo-diesel under the bonnet. It lends itself to any use, whether road, off-road, or competition, and has an innovatory system of disconnectable rear anti-roll bar.*

▲ *The pick-up's interior is well-equipped and car-like, even if the styling is a generation behind.*

▲ ▶ *The Terrano II is now just known as the Terrano, and can be specified with the Patrol's 3-litre 156bhp turbo-diesel.*

◀ *The interior of the Terrano has been spruced up, and can offer acres of leather and dummy wood, if that's your thing.*

▼ *The Hilux in its current form has been snappily restyled and given a spruced-up interior; single-cab, extended-cab and double-cab bodies are available, and power comes from a modern diesel, the 102bhp D4-D unit.*

▲ *The RAV4 did much to initiate a new class of small SUVs, and stood out for its excellent on-road comportment. The new version, launched in 2000, has either petrol or diesel engines and – whisper it! – is also available in 2wd.*

▲ *In tune with its exterior, the interior of the RAV4 is youthful, original and sporting in flavour. The electric windows, air-con and airbags are only to be expected these days; adjustable, folding and removable rear seats are another feature.*

▲ *The petrol version (without the bonnet air-scoop) uses a 147bhp 16-valve unit with variable valve timing. The four-door now accounts for most sales.*

The ever-present Toyota

Japan's Number One has always been a key player in the 4wd field – and a market-leader in some markets, such as France – thanks to its much-loved Land Cruiser and latterly the RAV4 sports-utility that was launched in 1994.

Now in its second generation, the RAV4 (also available in some markets with just front-wheel drive) was joined by a new Land Cruiser for the 2003 model year – although it had already been seen in the States as the Lexus GX470; the long-wheelbase Land Cruiser Amazon, otherwise known as the LC100, was also given a facelift to become the HDJ100, and received a new common-rail direct-injection 4.2-litre diesel engine as an alternative to its 4.7-litre petrol V8.

The Hilux pick-ups have also benefited from a new common-rail diesel, and have been spruced up in order to offer stronger competition to the L200 Mitsubishi.

The Lexus brand, meanwhile, is less readily associated with 4x4s in Europe, as a result of concentrating on the RX300 soft-roader alongside its saloons. A rival for the M-Class and the X5, the RX300 has recently had a full restyle, and has abandoned its estate-car format for a crossover coupé-estate look with a more raked rear; power continues to be from a 3.0-litre petrol V6 on European-market models, but a hybrid petrol-electric RX400H is on the horizon.

▲ The Land Cruiser is the direct descendant of the old BJ. These two versions, in lwb and swb form, have been replaced by a new range – although at a glance you'd be hard-pressed to tell them apart. The Lexus GX470 (below right) premiered the new look.

▲ The Land Cruiser has come a long way in a short time, in terms of its interior décor: it's now full-equipment luxury as standard. This is the last-generation car.

▲ The biggest Toyota 4x4 is the Amazon, powered by a choice of two hefty engines: a 235bhp 4.7-litre petrol V8 or a thumping 4.2-litre straight-six diesel developing 201bhp. A modest facelift arrived for 2003; this is the earlier version.

▲ With a 9ft 4in wheelbase, the Amazon has room for three rows of seats – with no shortage of comfort, thanks to air suspension all-round.

▲ ◀ The current GX470/Land Cruiser has dusted-over lines that echo those of the second-generation RAV4; two wheelbase lengths are available.

▲ The current Land Cruiser has either a 3-litre twin-cam four-cylinder turbo-diesel developing 161bhp or a 245bhp 4-litre petrol V6. A coil-sprung live back axle is retained.

▲ The rearmost seats on the new Land Cruiser fold up laterally, as with the previous model – and as the original Land Rover Discovery.
▼ The US-market Lexus GX470 has all the wood-effect trim you'd expect; best close your eyes and instead appreciate the creamy power of that lovely V8, a masterpiece of engineering derived from the unit first seen in the big Lexus saloons.

▼ The RX300 (or Toyota Harrier in Japan) was the first 'high-boy' crossover 4x4 – and the latest version, with its fastback rear, is even more split-identity.

◀ The RX300 has all the bells and whistles, and its interior is impressively high-grade, leather upholstery included; Mercedes and BMW can do no better.

▲ The old gang: the HZJ-75s have beam axles on leaf springs, and are still made in South Africa. With a six-cylinder 4.2-litre diesel they deliver an impressive thump.

▲ The Land Cruiser 105 is a savvy hybrid of the old HDJ-80 and the more recent LC 100 – it has the rigid axles of the former and the body of the latter. The Africans love them!

Available here!

▲ *The Romanian Aro now uses a 1.9-litre Renault turbo-diesel; a full range includes a four-door estate and a pick-up. Styling has been modified a little since this photo was taken.*

▼ *The only French 4x4, the Auverland is a truly competent off-roader, in line with the chamois motif on its badge; power comes from a 92bhp Peugeot turbo-diesel.*

There are countless 4x4 marques across the world. Some have been around for years, while others are relative newcomers. Suzuki, for example, has been present for decades, while Daihatsu was an early entry in the workhorse sector. Another old favourite is Lada: although the Niva is no longer sold in the UK, it continues to be available in some countries on mainland Europe. Equally long-lived is the Renault-engined Romanian ARO, which is again still available on the continent.

More mainstream is Isuzu, thanks to its association with General Motors, which saw its Rodeo pick-up being produced with Vauxhall and Opel badges for sale in Europe. The Isuzu also formed the basis for the first Vauxhall/Opel 4wd, the Frontera, made until 2003 in England.

Rather a different role is occupied by Subaru, whose characteristic 'boxer'-engined all-drive saloons, estates and pick-ups first became available in Europe in the early 1970s. The pick-ups have disappeared now, and the saloon and semi-estate Imprezas have become fashionable boy-racer wear on the back of the marque's rally successes, but Subaru hasn't forgotten its outdoors-y roots, and in the Forester offers a 4wd estate car of quiet off-road ability.

Honda came late to 4x4s – at one stage all it offered was a Japanese-market version of the Land Rover Discovery, carrying a Honda badge. But since then it has come up with the CR-V, and the more tarmac-orientated HR-V. In the States Honda additionally offers the bigger US-built Pilot SUV, together with an up-market Acura version called the MDX.

Meanwhile the major European firms have also continued to dabble in the softer end of the SUV market, notable examples being Renault's 4x4 versions of the Kangoo and Scénic.

◄ *Chevrolet's Trailblazer is the marque's latest mid-size SUV. With Auto-Trac permanent 4wd and a 4.2-litre straight-six developing 273bhp, this is a European-market version.*

▼ *The cheapest and most humble European 4x4 for many years was the Steyr-developed four-wheel-drive version of the Fiat Panda. By the time of publication the new Panda will be available in 4wd format.*

▼ *The Terios is something of an oddball, with its tallboy looks, but its light weight and lockable centre diff make the 1.3-litre permanent-4wd Daihatsu a game performer off-road, helped by its narrow girth.*

▲ *The Ford Ranger is also sold as the Mazda B-2500; 2wd and 4wd versions are offered, with a choice of cab configurations, and power comes from a 109bhp 2.5-litre turbo-diesel.*

▲ *The Isuzu Trooper, which has also been sold with Vauxhall and Opel badges, was the first 4x4 to have a common-rail direct-injection diesel. For comfort, off-road ability and carrying capacity the Trooper has a lot going for it – whether in 159bhp 3-litre diesel or 215bhp 3.5-litre petrol V6 form.*

The Lada Niva is the only long-term European success story for the former USSR: in production since 1978, the stubby permanent-4wd three-door estate has carved its own niche as a car-like compact off-roader of undisputed ruggedness.

▲ The second-generation Honda CRV has the same range of virtues as its progenitor – it's just a bit bigger and a bit more powerful.

▶ The Frontera was launched in 1991 and restyled in 1996. Made in Britain, it was discontinued at the end of 2003; both three-door and five-door versions were offered, with a 2.2-litre diesel or a V6 3.2-litre petrol engine.

◀ Renault's Kangoo is available with 4wd, adding to the versatility of this cheeky van-derived estate; both petrol and diesel engines are available.

▼ The Samurai is Suzuki's original 4x4, and can trace its lineage back to the 800cc LJ20 Jimny of 1972. Basic and harsh-riding (on tarmac), it is an excellent off-roader. The last European versions had a 1.3-litre petrol or a 1.9-litre turbo-diesel.

▲ The Mazda Tribute got caught up in Ford's purchase of Land Rover, and soon disappeared off the map, along with its badge-engineered sister, the Ford Maverick, in favour of the Land Rover Freelander. Power comes from a 2-litre 'four' or 3-litre V6, both these being petrol engines.

▼ The Renault Scénic RX4 had all the virtues of the company's trendsetting MPV, plus permanent 4wd and a low-ratio transfer box. The exterior spare wheel and the plastic body cladding are recognition points.

▲ The Subaru Forester is a bit of a dark horse. Shame the US-market 2.5-litre isn't Euro-available: for that you'll have to go for the Legacy estate or its pumped-up Outback sister, both of which are also available with a tasty 3-litre flat-six.

▼ The Jimny is a modernised Samurai, with coil springs all-round – still with solid axles. The engine is a 1.3 petrol unit, although in some markets a 1.5 turbo-diesel is available.

▼ Middle of the Suzuki 4x4 range, the Vitara has a 1.6-litre petrol engine or a 2-litre Peugeot turbo-diesel.

▲ The Grand Vitara is the ultimate development of the Vitara, and in lwb five-door form is available with a 184bhp 2736cc petrol V6 or a 109bhp 1997cc Peugeot Hdi diesel. A high-low transfer box aids off-road performance.

▶ *Created in association with Volkswagen, Porsche's Cayenne S is no blushing flower, with its 340bhp 4.5-litre V8 (with 310lb ft of torque at 2500rpm) giving it a 150mph maximum speed; the Turbo version, with its gaping side vents, is good for close-on 160mph on its 450bhp.*

▲ *The Allroad range-topper is a 4.2-litre V8 developing 300bhp; other engines are a twin-turbo 250bhp 2.7-litre V6 and a 180bhp 2.5-litre V6 turbo-diesel.*

▲ *Cayennes have a six-speed manual or a Tiptronic six-speed automatic. The lavish equipment includes the inevitable sat-nav, part of the PCM ('Porsche Communication Management') system that also takes in the carphone, TV and heating. There's more room than an M-Class but less than in a Range Rover.*

▲ *Derived from the AAC prototype displayed at the 2000 Detroit show, the Touareg shares its platform and centre section with the Cayenne; power comes from VW's 3.2-litre staggered-vee V6, or either a five-cylinder or V10 diesel.*
▼ *Air springs are optional on the Cayenne V6 and the S and standard on the Turbo. Permanent 4wd has a 38/62 front/rear split in normal use; Porsche Traction Management electronically controls this distribution and the locking of the centre differential.*

The European offensive

Looking back, it seems inevitable that those European manufacturers not at the time making off-roaders would sooner or later decide that they weren't going to leave the field to the Japanese or to Land Rover any longer. The surprise is, though, that some of the most unlikely marques have gone 4x4 – and yet they haven't damaged their brand values.

BMW led the way, with the X5 of 1999, made in its Spartanburg factory in the US and managing to combine off-road competence with traditional BMW standards of roadholding and ride on tarmac. Given its immediate success, it is no great shock that BMW has subsequently launched a smaller off-roader, the X3 – although it should be pointed out that there's in fact not that much difference between the two models in either size or price.

Volvo was next off the blocks, with its XC90 of 2002, designed in the US and with two-thirds of its sales expected to be in the States. Intentionally more car-like and less aggressive than some other 4x4s, the XC90 nevertheless manages to fit seven seats into its relatively modest overall size.

The Volkswagen group was until recently too busy indulging in vanity projects such as Bugatti and Bentley to pay more than cursory attention to the 4x4 market: the best it could manage was the 'soft-road' Audi Allroad, a jacked-up A6 estate. But a slice of the lucrative US market for SUVs ultimately proved irresistible, and the result was a joint-venture with Porsche. This has spawned the VW Touareg and the most improbable Porsche of all time, the Cayenne, both on sale from 2003. Those not choking on their bratwurst will doubtless be comforted by the fatboy Porsche pumping out 450bhp in top-of-range twin-turbo V8 form; Touareg owners, meanwhile, have to content themselves with a 313bhp V10 bi-turbo diesel in the top model. When the Germans come out to play they don't take prisoners…

▲ *With its vee'd bonnet and pronounced shoulders, the XC90 conforms to the house style established by design chief Peter Horbury. The Volvo is a capable rival to the BMW X5 and has been a great sales success.*

▲ Top-of-range X5s have a V8; initially this was a 4.4-litre or (as here) 4.6-litre unit, but now the larger engine is a 4.8-litre unit.

▲ The Audi Allroad benefits from an optional low-range gearbox on the V6s (but not the V8); all models have height-adjustable suspension.

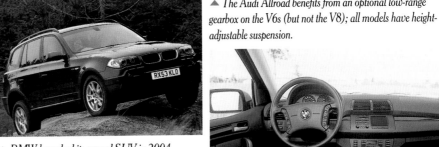

▲ BMW launched its second SUV in 2004, initially only with petrol engines but with two diesels promised for the future. The X3 features xDrive full-time 4wd, set up to give a 68:32 power bias to the rear in normal driving and linked to the Dynamic Stability Control system.

▼ The Touareg has all the interior quality you'd expect of Volkswagen. The Tiptronic gearbox, when fitted, has steering-wheel controls; the alternative is a six-speed manual.

▲ Audi is a past master when it comes to interior fit and finish, and the Allroad 4.2-litre V8 is no exception to the rule, with its well-conceived and luxurious cockpit.

▲ The X5's interior, in its original form: latest versions have been sharpened up a little, to accompany more in-depth changes, such as the new xDrive 4wd system.

▲ The VW Touareg has different suspension settings from those of the Cayenne; air springs are standard on the V10.

▲ As well as the V8s, in-line petrol (231bhp) and diesel (218bhp) six-cylinder engines are available on the X5.

◀ The XC90 has a choice of five-in-line 210bhp or straight-six 272bhp turbocharged petrol engines, or the 2.4-litre 163bhp D5 turbo-diesel; all are transversely mounted. The chassis, derived from that of the S70/V70 and S80, incorporates RSC electronic Roll Stability Control, and all but the five-cylinder petrol car have adaptive automatic transmission as standard.

▶ The Volvo interior has a cool scandinavian style and includes a Dolby Pro Logic II sound system. With the extra third row of seats it can accommodate up to seven people.

The Koreans: back in strength

▲ *For a long time a Korean 4x4 meant the Hyundai Galloper, a development of the first-generation Mitsubishi Shogun available in some European countries but never sold in Britain.*

▲ *The British-styled Korando began life as a Ssangyong, was subsequently badged as a Daewoo, and is now back under its original name.*

Battered by the storms of the financial crisis in Asia at the end of the 1990s, the Korean marques have now bounced back, thanks to a round of industrial reorganisation and calmer financial waters. But survival had its price, and meant either withdrawing from the market in some instances or striking up alliances in the case of others. Thus the end of 1998 saw Kia come under the control of Hyundai, to form the biggest Korean firm, while Ssangyong and Daewoo came together, and are now under the General Motors umbrella after GM took control in 2000.

Since then there have been countless new products, not least various 4x4s, and a slew of modern diesel engines. Leading the way was Hyundai, who in 2000 announced its first 4x4, the Santa Fe; this soft-roader estate has been a great success, helped by the 2.0-litre common-rail diesel that is offered alongside the usual four-cylinder and V6 petrol engines.

More recently there has been the 2.9-litre turbo-diesel Terracan, Hyundai's pitch at the Shogun/Patrol market. With selectable 4wd, a low-ratio gearbox and a limited-slip differential, its off-road credentials aren't in doubt; it is effectively a replacement for the Galloper, a second-generation Shogun made under licence by Hyundai.

Over at Daewoo the Ssangyong Korando and Musso have been seen with the Daewoo badge, but have been somewhat eclipsed by the Rexton, a hefty 4x4 aimed at the Mercedes M-Class and the BMW X5: at which the Korean newcomer takes a fair pop.

Finally Kia has brought out its own contender in this up-market sector, with its Sorrento, built on the same platform as the Hyundai Terracan and clearly apeing the Mercedes in its styling. Power comes from a modern common-rail diesel or a 3.5-litre petrol V6, with a 2.4-litre petrol 'four' additionally available in some countries.

▲ *The Korando's strong points include its Mercedes-derived engines and its competitive pricing; three-door, van and soft-top versions are available. Power units include a 3199cc petrol straight-six, which on 220bhp makes the Korando a 120mph car.*

▲ *The Korando's sister is the Musso long-wheelbase estate; again the engines are Mercedes-based. Not seen in Europe is a handy-looking double-cab pick-up version.*

▲ *The Rexton is a big muscular device that still uses Mercedes-derived power units, straight-six included; the styling is better than on some Korean 4x4s.*

▼ *The interior is competently designed and well-equipped, making the Rexton an attractive buy at the price; the UK-market cars use a five-cylinder 2.9 diesel or the 3.2-litre petrol 'six' and are sold under the Ssangyong name.*

▲ *The interior is certainly spacious, and blessed with a decent boot. A seven-seater with a third row of seats is available.*

▲ The 3.2-litre develops 217bhp; the permanent 4wd is mated to a low-high transfer box and there is an electronic diff lock.

▲ The Kia Sportage has been around since the early 1990s and is a neat Freelander-class vehicle, available with both petrol and diesel engines.

▲ Alongside the five-door estate a more sporting two-door with an open rear is manufactured. When fitted with the 128bhp twin-cam 2-litre engine it flies along.

▲ The Kia Sorento is built on the same platform as the Hyundai Terracan. The diesel engine is a direct-injection common-rail unit developing 140bhp.

▶ The Santa Fe is an SUV aimed at the mildly off-road crossover-class Japanese such as the Subaru Forester and Mitsubishi Outlander; there's no transfer box or diff-lock.

▲ The Sorento has top-level interior trim and equipment, including sat-nav. Performance to match? Go for the 3.5-litre V6 variant, which offers 195bhp…

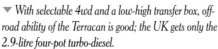

▲ The Terracan rings the changes, being more of an off-roader than its Kia sister; suspension is all-independent.

▼ With selectable 4wd and a low-high transfer box, off-road ability of the Terracan is good; the UK gets only the 2.9-litre four-pot turbo-diesel.

▲ The Hyundai Santa Fe scores with a more spacious interior than its rivals, and its equipment and finish can't be reproached; the auto gearbox has a sequential mode.

▼ Three engine are available in the Santa Fe: a 2.4-litre petrol 'four', a petrol 2656cc V6, and a common-rail direct-injection 115bhp turbo-diesel.

The USA: mother country for the 4x4

▲ *The Cadillac Escalade EXT is GM's answer to the Lincoln Blackwood. Based on the Chevrolet Avalanche, it uses a 6-litre V8 but can only manage a 13.8cwt payload. Still, the rigid cover for the pick-up bed is neat…*

▲ *The Chevrolet Silverado is the second-best-selling pick-up in the US, and is GM's full-size warhorse, available in various wheelbase and cab configurations; engines are V6 or V8, including a V8 turbo-diesel.*

The United States is the place on the planet with the greatest concentration of 4x4s, with a particular emphasis on pick-ups. Having been around in the US pretty much since the dawn of motoring, pick-ups are part of the American scenery, as workhorses as much as recreational playthings. The full-size version – think Ford F150, for example – is an American staple, but below it are more manageably-sized vehicles, some of which began life, in earlier incarnations, as Japanese imports.

The Japanese have remained strong players, but are now firmly implanted as US-based constructors: Nissan, Toyota, Isuzu and Mazda pick-ups for the US are all locally built. Until recently they kept to compact-sized models, but they are now moving into the full-size sector, previously the preserve of the American 'Big Three'. Already Toyota's Tundra and Nissan's Titan have their feet under the star-spangled table, and Honda is readying its own full-sizer.

Under attack from the Japanese on one side and from the prestige European makes on the other, the US manufacturers are fighting back in two ways: on the one hand with more innovative products, and on the other with models that bring the 4x4 to top-line brands who had previously turned their back on 'redneck' trucks.

In the former category are vehicles such as the oddball Pontiac Aztek or the rather more normal Pontiac Vibe, which is basically a US-built Toyota Corolla Verso in drag, and Ford's double-cab Explorer Sport Trac recreational pick-up with its ingenious expandable load-deck. In the latter category, count such taste-free glitzmobiles as the Cadillac Escalade, the Mercury Mountaineer and the Lincoln Navigator. Based on lesser Ford or GM products, it's difficult to see whom these things fool, but the bean-counters must approve, as the latest off the block is a dolled-up Chevrolet truck badged as a Saab.

◀ *The second series of Cadillac Escalade remains a facelifted Chevrolet Tahoe, and is powered by a 285bhp or 345bhp V8. The GMC Yukon is basically the same thing, too.*

▲ *The truck-sized Chevrolet HD3500 has twin rear wheels and is over 20ft long; it's more workhorse than recreational vehicle.*

▲ *The Chevrolet Avalanche is essentially a tricked-up Silverado for the leisure market; for extra carrying capacity the bulkhead between the interior and the pick-up bed can be folded down.*

▲ *The Chevrolet Suburban is the latest of a line going back to 1937, and is Chevy's no-nonsense full-size truck-based estate. Engine range from a 5.3-litre V8 to a massive 8.1-litre unit delivering 320bhp and 440lbs ft of torque.*

◀ *The Dodge Dakota is the pick-up version of the mid-size Durango sports-utility, and comes with a regular, extended or double cabin; engines range from a 120bhp four-cylinder through a V6 to the inevitable V8, here a 5.9-litre unit developing 250bhp.*

▲ *Daimler-Chrysler's big-boy pick-up is the Dodge Ram, again available with a choice of three cabins. Engines are a 5.9-litre in-line turbo-diesel 'six', a 3.9-litre petrol V6, a brace of V8s, or a stump-pulling 310bhp 8-litre V10.*

▼ *The Yukon XL is the GMC version of the Chevy Tahoe, and the Denali shown here is the most luxurious model. Engines available are a 285bhp 5.3-litre V8, a 300bhp or 325bhp 6.0-litre V8, and a 340bhp 8.1-litre V8.*

▲ *Underneath its gussied-up exterior the Mercury Mountaineer is nothoing more than a mid-size Ford Explorer. Power comes from a 210bhp 4.0-litre V6 or a 240bhp 4.6-litre V8.*

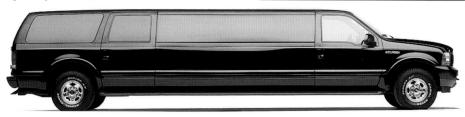

▲ *Presumably endowed with the rigidity of an overripe banana, this extended limousine version of the Ford Excursion can be kitted out to suit the customer. It measures 31ft long and weighs nearly 4 tons.*

▲ *Mid-size SUV sisters from GM: to the left the GMC Envoy, to the right the Chevrolet TrailBlazer…and lurking backstage the Oldsmobile Bravada, yet another badge-engineered Olds that failed to revive America's oldest car brand, which finally disappeared in 2004.*

▲ *The Expedition is Ford's full-size SUV equivalent to the Chevrolet Tahoe, and is powered by either a 215bhp 4.6-litre V8 or a bigger 5.4-litre unit developing 264bhp.*

▼ *For more than 20 years the Ford F-Series has been the best-selling vehicle in the States: versions offered include the F150, F250 and F350 in a range extending all the way to an enormous F750.*

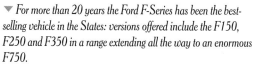

▲ *The Navigator is the first 4x4 offered by Ford's premier Lincoln brand, and under the Lincoln disguise it is a Ford Expedition. Main competitor is the Cadillac Escalade.*

▶ *Unveiled as a concept car in 2001, the neat Scénic-sized Pontiac Vibe has been available from 2002; power comes from a 125bhp Toyota 'four'.*

▲ *Meanwhile, the luxury pick-up side of the market is being attacked by the Lincoln Blackwood, with its plush double-cab interior. It's more Los Angeles than Appalachian backwoods.*

▶ *The Buick Rendezvous is a compact SUV with a 3.4-litre V6 of 185bhp and a 4wd system without low-range gearing; it is aimed at the Lexus RX300 and the like.*

▲ *Honda does a two-hander in the States, offering the Pilot SUV under its own name and the related MDX as an up-market Acura; both are made in Canada and use a 3471cc V6 developing 243bhp; full-time 4wd and a variable torque split feature.*

▲ *The Lexus LX470 is nothing more than a gussied-up Land Cruiser, but benefits from a 230bhp 4.7-litre V8.*

▲ *The United States saw the latest Toyota Land Cruiser early, in the shape of the Lexus GX470 – complete with a creamy 238bhp 4.7-litre V8 engine as standard.*

▲ *The GX470 has a spacious interior and all the toys, such as sat-nav and a five-speed auto.*

▼ *The star-turn in its class, the Lexus RX300 has turned into a real Stateside love-affair since its launch in 1999, especially among urban trendies. Only a 204bhp 2995cc V6 is available.*

Under the star-spangled banner

For some years now the American 'Big Three' – Ford, GM and Chrysler – have been under attack from the Japanese, and latterly from the Germans. In fact it's true to say that the old-guard US manufacturers have caught a cold. They have been forced into lay-offs, re-structurings and product rationalisation, yet have failed to prevent the newcomers from becoming established.

All the Japanese majors have set up plants in the US, with or without tie-ins with American firms, and so also have BMW and Mercedes. Long gone, too, is the idea of the Japanese as producers of cheap little runabouts, all the key players having set up their own luxury brands – Infiniti at Nissan, Acura at Honda, and of course Lexus at Toyota. Unsurprisingly, given that SUVs and pick-ups account for half the US market (which absorbed 16.6m vehicles in 2003), all three of these brands have their own 4x4s – not least Lexus, who pioneered the crossover genre with its RX300. As for the Germans, the BMW X5 and Mercedes M-Class hardly need any introduction...

Dial in those models carrying the badge of familiar US makes but in reality locally-built versions of Japanese vehicles, and you have a fascinatingly diverse market.

▷ *Specially designed for the US market, the sleek Isuzu Axiom has a four-speed auto and 2wd or full-time 4wd. It would be nice to see it in Europe...*

◁ *Nissan's prestige Infiniti brand is only sold in the US and Canada, and offers two 4x4s, the QX56 and the crossover coupé-estate FX (in V6 and V8 forms); this is the QX56, which has a 5.6-litre V8 of 313bhp.*

▲ *The Suzuki Grand Vitara XL-7 is a stretched version essentially conceived for the US; for European markets the 2.7-litre V6 is supplemented by a 1997cc Peugeot turbo-diesel.*

▲ *The Canadian Catvee is a Hummer rip-off based on a General Motors chassis and mechanicals. But it's lighter than the original – by about a ton! – and much cheaper, especially if you buy it as a kit for converting an existing GM truck.*

▲ *The Nissan Murano interior is particularly well thought-out; an 'intelligent' automatic is standard, as is an on-board computer with sat-nav. European sales are just beginning.*

▲ *The Nissan X-Terra is a US-built low-price SUV, based on the Frontier pick-up – so it's a low-frills device with a leaf-sprung rear axle and 4wd as an extra-cost option. With the X-Terra, Nissan has aimed for the youth market, where fancy kit is less important than functional fittings and affordability.*

▲ *With Mercedes pumping out the M-Class, BMW was never going to sit on its hands, and in 2000 the first X5s left its Spartanburg plant in South Carolina. Power comes from straight-sixes (petrol and diesel) and V8s.*

▲ *Nissan's riposte to the crossover RX300 has been the Murano, launched in 2003. With optional full-time 4wd and a 245bhp 3.5-litre V6, it should cope with getting its boots dirty; Euro sales started in 2004.*

▲ *The Chevrolet Tracker is a re-badged Canadian-built Suzuki Grand Vitara, the Japanese firm being a part-owned affiliate of General Motors.*

◀▲▲*Mercedes was the first European maker to produce a 4x4 in the States, when it set up a factory in Tuscsaloosa, Alabama, to produce the ML, on sale since 1997. The range-topping AMG 55 is much coveted…*

Techniques
and
practicalities

▼ *Vehicles with selectable 4wd are often fitted with freewheel front hubs, which can be either manually or electrically operated. These allow the transmission to be disconnected from the wheels when the vehicle is used on the road in 2wd format.*

▲ *Sometimes the central differential of full-time 4x4s is of the Torsen torque-sensing variable-slip type; sometimes it is replaced by a viscous coupling, generally electronically-controlled.*

Because of the use to which they are put, and because of the background from which they have come, 4x4s tend to have a different technical make-up from a regular passenger car – above all in terms of chassis, suspension and transmission. Take a look at the spec sheets in the brochures and you'll soon appreciate the differences, and get an idea about what is important for your needs.

Without drowning in the detail, let's look at the basics. The classic configuration is a rear-wheel-drive vehicle onto which a 2wd/4wd transfer box has been grafted, attached to the gearbox, so that drive can be taken to the front wheels by actuating a second lever beside the normal gearlever. The next step in evolution, represented in the UK by the 1970 Range Rover, was to make the 4wd permanent. This however meant that on high-adhesion surfaces – in other words on normal tarmac roads – one set of wheels over-ran the other; to counter this problem it was necessary to fit a central differential, to compensate for the fact that the front wheels were rotating at a different rate from the rear wheels.

Part of the gearbox assembly is the reduction gearing, which reduces each gear ratio by roughly a half. Control of the reduction gearing is generally incorporated in the same transfer box as effects the change between 2wd and 4wd, and will be controlled by the same lever – although a Willys Jeep or a leaf-sprung Land Rover, for example, will have a separate lever for both functions.

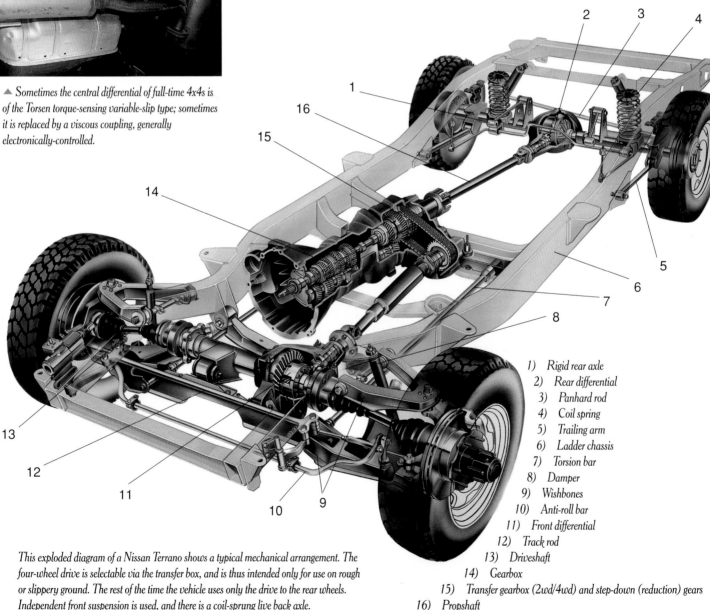

1) Rigid rear axle
2) Rear differential
3) Panhard rod
4) Coil spring
5) Trailing arm
6) Ladder chassis
7) Torsion bar
8) Damper
9) Wishbones
10) Anti-roll bar
11) Front differential
12) Track rod
13) Driveshaft
14) Gearbox
15) Transfer gearbox (2wd/4wd) and step-down (reduction) gears
16) Propshaft

This exploded diagram of a Nissan Terrano shows a typical mechanical arrangement. The four-wheel drive is selectable via the transfer box, and is thus intended only for use on rough or slippery ground. The rest of the time the vehicle uses only the drive to the rear wheels. Independent front suspension is used, and there is a coil-sprung live back axle.

These are the main types of suspension found on 4 x 4s.

▶ *Independent front suspension by double wishbones and longitudinal torsion bars: less common, but there's nothing wrong with such a set-up, which has the advantage of feeding suspension stresses into the strong central crossmember of the chassis.*

▲ *Independent front suspension by unequal-length wishbones and coil springs, here with the dampers concentric with the coil springs. Double-wishbone suspension gives the best wheel location.*

▶ *Independent front suspension using MacPherson struts. Essentially private-car practice, it is cheap, reasonably effective, but wheel location is less satisfactory.*

▶ *Beam rear axle with coil springs: a robust system which offers constant ground clearance and is very common on 4x4s. Shown is a lift-kitted vehicle with twin dampers either side; the diagonal bar is a Panhard Rod, to give lateral location to the axle.*

▲ *Live back axle on leaf springs – you can't get more traditional than this. Found on most pick-ups, it copes well with heavy loads but gives a more abrupt ride and less satisfactory axle location.*

▲ *Increasingly the traditional separate ladder frame has found itself replaced by monocoque construction – reflecting the demands for 4x4s to become less truck-like in on-road use. The result is a more rigid and lighter-weight structure.*

▶ *The Shogun transmission illustrates the various permutations made possible by the transfer gearbox.*
2H: rear-wheel drive ('2 High') only. For road use.
4H: four-wheel drive ('4 High') with centre diff operational. Can be used on the road, eg in slippery conditions.
4H Lc: four-wheel drive, with centre diff locked ('4 High Locked centre'). Off-road use only.
4L Lc: four-wheel drive with diff locked and low-ratio gearing engaged ('4 Low Locked centre'). Off-road use only, with gearing reduced by roughly a half.

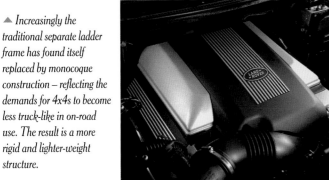

◀ *Engines specially adapted for 4x4s tend to have certain specific features. The crankshaft counterweights are more substantial, so that their added inertia increases low-range torque and thus low-speed flexibility; the sump is baffled, to help retain oil when the vehicle is on a slope; the bearings, pulleys and shafts are given better seals to withstand mud, sand and even snow more effectively.*

Off-roading: getting it right

▲▼ *The bigger the maximum angles of approach and departure of a 4x4, the better its off-road abilities will be.*

The 4x4 can be both a sublimely efficient piece of locomotion and an object of something approaching ridicule. Here's what I mean. Take a serious 4x4, and you can tackle climbs and descents so steep your passengers will be shaking. Yet that same 4x4 could find itself ignominiously stuck in the mildest of mudholes or rough terrain, with those same passengers mocking the driver for having got them into such a daft situation. To avoid that sort of humiliation, and to avoid unfair criticism of the poor 4x4 itself, you really should, for reasons of safety and commonsense, take the time to learn a few simple and effective rules.

These begin with setting the seat further forward than normal, so that you're not left hanging onto the wheel on the slighest climb. You'll also find that arm movements are easier. Similarly, for repeated applications of lock, which you're bound to encounter, it's better to forget the ten-to-ten position of your hands on the wheel, in favour of a twenty-past-eight position that will help with the lower-geared steering that is normal on 4x4s.

The other key attribute is anticipation. Once faced with the obstacle to be overcome, you need to look ahead to the point of exit, and even to the next obstacle, if you can see that far. In fact, it's always a sensible idea to get out of the car and reconnoitre a little, so you don't have any nasty surprises.

Finally, at the beginning of the exercise engage four-wheel drive – or engage the centre diff lock on a full-time 4wd vehicle. Don't forget to disengage the diff lock – and the 4wd if applicable – when you're back on tarmac.

The photos illustrate some of the key challenges you are likely to face.

▼ *By the same token, side clearance is crucial – you'll really be handicapped if it is insufficient. Not only that, but you risk damaging your sills.*

▼ *A climb should always be in the direction of the slope, and never across it – especially if the incline is steep. Otherwise, you risk turning the car over. Use of the low-range gears is obligatory, and you should keep your feet off the clutch, even if that means you stall.*

▼*It is always a good idea to get out and reconnoitre if you don't have a clear view ahead, so you can assess, for example, the extent of the slope or the depth of a stretch of water.*

▶ *This is what happens if you tackle a descent crossways. In this situation a bit of throttle would save the day, by putting the vehicle back on four wheels and restoring directional ability. But brake sharply, and the weight of the 4x4 would take over, and the car would roll.*

▲ *Downhill sections are tackled in low-ratio second or first – feet off the clutch! The vehicle is slowed on its brakes, but without stopping it dead and always in the direction of the slope. If you move off-course, it is better to accelerate to get back on line rather than to brake, which will exacerbate the drift.*

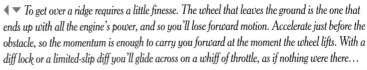

▲▼ To get over a ridge requires a little finesse. The wheel that leaves the ground is the one that ends up with all the engine's power, and so you'll lose forward motion. Accelerate just before the obstacle, so the momentum is enough to carry you forward at the moment the wheel lifts. With a diff lock or a limited-slip diff you'll glide across on a whiff of throttle, as if nothing were there...

▼ A gulley is best attacked diagonally, so that the suspension travel works most efficiently in your favour, in other words one wheel after the other.

▼ If you end up tilting sideways, as here, you have to be careful – and a novice often has completely the wrong reflex. If you start to lose grip, you must steer down the slope, not up it – otherwise you'll soon be on the phone to your favourite body-shop!

▼ Emerging diagonally from a gulley means that you won't always have all four wheels on the ground. Be careful not to land the airborne wheel with an over-enthusiastic use of the throttle, otherwise you'll risk breaking a halfshaft.

▲ If grip is poor, such as in sand or mud, you can reduce tyre pressures to maybe 15psi. Traction will be substantially increased.

▼ Fording a stream or river can mean ending up with a wrecked engine...or an impromptu swim. For heaven's sake investigate before you take the plunge, and if there's more than a foot and a half of water then watch out, as water is likely to get in through the air-filter intake. Best proceed at a regular speed, making a bow wave.

▼ Don't hesitate to lean out of the window and see what the wheels are doing. A low beltline (on the car...) is helpful here, as is the fact that some 4x4s have the driver's seat close to the door.

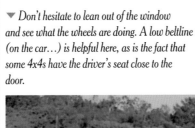

▲ In a bog like this, or in any conditions of low grip, when the wheels start to spin you should avoid the natural reflex of trying to accelerate out of trouble: you'll only dig yourself in deeper. Back off the throttle, and finding a bit of grip will be easier.

▲ Decent wheel travel on a 4x4 is a key attribute, allowing the wheels to stay in contact with the ground for as long as possible, and thus ensure maximum traction.

▲ *It might date from the 1940s, but driving a Willys Jeep is always a real blast.*

We love you!

As someone who has been testing cars for a living for some few years, the author is aware how passion, even if it's still there, deep down, can somehow level out into a more emotionless acceptance. Until, that is, the day when you come across a vehicle so beguiling that you can't get it out of your mind for a good six months. With an off-roader it could be a top-of-range 4x4 or something basic, a straight-forward SUV or a piece of competition machinery. This affection could be a result of your state of mind at the time, the place where you happen to be – or the people you're with, maybe.

This selection, which is totally arbitrary and by no means exhaustive, does I hope reflect, all the same, the hidden qualities of some off-roaders, qualities you can't quantify with a computer or any other measuring tool. And if this works for me, why not for you?

The Willys Jeep is the perfect example of what I mean. Some fall in love with this most rudimentary of 4x4s because it brings the past alive for them, on a wave of nostalgia – for example in the case of those who learnt to drive on a Jeep during military service, or in the case of those who saw the Jeep on French roads for the first time during the summer of '44.

As far as I'm concerned, I first drove a Jeep pretty late in my professional life, when I was doing an article on fire-break tracks in the Landes. So there was no nostalgia kick for me, but ever since that day I've grabbed the chance to drive that goddamned Jeep again! It's the most stripped-to-the-bone thing I've ever experienced, with not an ounce of sophistication, but at the wheel you just get a huge buzz from its sheer charisma.

All that, with just a seat, a steering wheel, an engine – and four lovely driven wheels…

▲ *The Hummer H2 follows the recipe of the Hummer H1, which is essentially a military vehicle, but brings much more to the party when it comes to 'civilian' use.*

▲ *Under its brutalist skin lies a frankly luxurious interior which all the same manages to echo the H2's carved-from-the-solid exterior lines – just clock that gearshift!*

▲ *Off-road, the traction control, the rear diff lock, the axle articulation and the sensational angles of attack and departure make this dinosaur a real ace when it comes to the rough stuff – just so long as it's been left enough room…*

◀ *The engine is a good old single-cam petrol V8, with electronic injection. With 316bhp and 569lb ft of torque, it's more fun than its turbo-diesel H1 brother.*

▲ *How could you fail to fall for the charms of this Toyota BJ42! Just a look and it conjures up a world of adventure, the wide open spaces of Africa, the very heart-and-soul of an off-roader.*
▼ *The interior pushes the same buttons. It's as if you're back in the 1960s, although this example dates from 1982 and production only ended in 1984.*

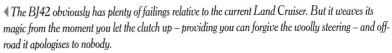
The BJ42 obviously has plenty of failings relative to the current Land Cruiser. But it weaves its magic from the moment you let the clutch up – providing you can forgive the woolly steering – and off-road it apologises to nobody.

▼ *Once an enthusiast gets hold of it, the VW Iltis can end up a superb recreational vehicle. It's well worth giving one a try.*

▲ *The Iltis is still quite something. Underneath that Amphicar look there's a multi-function motor car waiting to get out. With all-round independent suspension and its ultra-low first gear, its surprising comfort and its impressive angles of attack, the VW is a star off-roader.*

▼ *The Cherokee is fun, warm-hearted, and hot stuff on all surfaces, in its 190bhp six-cylinder form. Its replacement isn't bad, either…*

▲ *The Mercedes 'G' is completely bombproof. It's also the off-road king, so long as it's dry, thanks to its three diff locks. In the wet, its weight counts against it.*

▲ *An SUV in this selection? Sacrilege! But if the Nissan X-Trail is as happy on the road as a decent saloon, its suspension, DCi engine and locking central diff allow you to take some serious liberties off-road.*

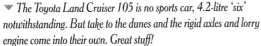
▼ *The Toyota Land Cruiser 105 is no sports car, 4.2-litre 'six' notwithstanding. But take to the dunes and the rigid axles and lorry engine come into their own. Great stuff!*

▲ *The Auverland is a little gem off-road. At the wheel, everything seems simple. With its crazy axle articulation and low centre of gravity, the lack of a diff lock really doesn't matter.*

▲ *The 5.9-litre V8 Grand Cherokee is the best of the US machinery, with its beefy torque-rich engine, its well-conceived suspension and its cool looks. How could you not fall for it?*

▶ *This Jeep Wrangler tries a bit of three-wheeling. With luck the driver came down without too much of a bang. This looks dramatic, but it also means that you've lost one driven wheel…which doesn't help forward motion.*

▼ *The Red Prince is only loosely related to a Jeep. It's one of the Iceland boys in action in downtown Swindon. Note the small sand tyres used on these Icelandic home-brews.*

Boys just want to have fun…

▲ *Nitrous oxide gives a huge boost to an already powerful engine, by adding oxygen to the fuel so that it burns more efficiently. But sometimes things can get out of hand, as in the case of this nitrous fire.*

▲ *Another one of the Icelanders in action, tackling a mudsplash. The drivers really are quite fearless in these contests.*

▲ *With this rig about to topple over, or so it appears, you can see the vehicle's square-tube construction, including the beefy suspension arms, and the near full-length skidplate.*

Off-roading can be serious – ask anyone competing at the top level. But it can also be a barrel of fun, whether you're taking part in a sporting event or just letting your hair down with a bunch of mates. Over the years the author has had a good few laughs along the way, met some crazy blokes, and in his work covered some hugely enjoyable events. He's also watched some people end up in situations in which they'd rather not have found themselves. Like in the middle of a mud hole, with no way of getting out…

This pictorial review covers some of the fun moments in off-roading. Before you laugh too much, ask yourself whether you'd be daft enough to get into some of these situations. Think before you get in too deep – and I mean that literally!

Kicking off, though, are some photos from one of the wackiest off-road competitions, the Icelandic Formula Off-Road series. Held in Iceland (as you might expect) but also in Norway and Sweden, this championship first came to prominence as the result of a British TV programme. It caught the public fancy, with the result that our Nordic friends came over to Swindon for a round of the series.

The cars used are tube-framed specials with power coming from V8s developing up to 800bhp on nitrous-oxide. Competing on volcanic shingle, these buggies really go for it, pulling spectacular wheelies and sometimes even turning over. It's pretty much the most extreme off-roading in the world.

Nothing to do with competition, but as far as mad-cap exploits are concerned trying out an amphibious Jeep in the middle of December takes some beating. To photograph the 'Seep' – as they are nicknamed – photographer and journalist had to break the ice on the Huddersfield canal before they could launch the device. Photo-shoot over, they then cruised the canal in this bizarre vehicle, complete with its machine gun… and somehow managed to avoid getting arrested.

▲ *Another Icelandic buggy waggles its two front wheels on a steep climb. The long-travel coil-spring suspension – on beam axles, of course – makes the cars relatives to the rock-crawlers found in the States.*

◀ *A reminder that one can make a fool of oneself in snow just as much as in mud. Trying to be just a little too clever, this Jeep driver is nicely embedded. It took until five o'clock the following morning to extricate him…*

▶ *Rather more decorously, this beautifully restored Series II Land Rover tackles a ford – a picture chosen as a counterpoint to all the mud-spattered goings-on elsewhere on these pages…and because the Landie looks such a honey.*

▶ *It pays to have shares in a washing-powder company if you do a lot of off-roading – or else a tolerant wife, girlfriend or local launderette. Getting down and dirty is what it's all about…*

▶ *This is how things go wrong: the Range Rover is stuck, and as so often the case, it's down to a good old swb Land Rover pick-up to pull matey onto terra firma. No reflection on the Range Rover – their off-road ability is second to none, thanks to their lovely long-travel suspension.*

◀ *The little Suzuki is very competent off-roader. It's light, agile and manoeuvrable, with rugged beam axles front and rear. But even so, you can get one stuck.*

▶ *A Jeep deep in the sticky stuff. Lots of wheel-churning suggests the plot is in danger of being lost, but as long as you are maintaining forward motion and putting the power down you should generally be able to pull yourself through. But once you've stalled or bogged, it's time for that tow-rope moment.*

▼ *Hold on tight chaps! This Jeep Wrangler is about to hit a typical mudhole, as usually arranged at events such as Jeep Jamborees. It's not unheard of for gung-ho antics such as this to end in tears – or at least in a thorough dunking.*

▼ *Talking of which, this Land Rover 90 seems to have its engine brewing nicely as it gets stuck in a mudhole during the SWROC Mendip Challenge, a friendly local club event.*

▲ *Catch 'em young! These junior jeepsters are keeping surprisingly clean, while in a bit of inspired role-reversal their dad is presumably paddling about in the mud somewhere stage right.*

▲ *The amphibious Jeep under way – on the Huddersfield canal. Strictly speaking called the GPA, it was nicknamed the Seep. Built on a longer wheelbase, it could be powered in the water either just by the propeller or – in an emergency – by using the wheels as well.*

▶ *To prevent the engine from being drowned by the bow-wave there was a hinge-down surf shield. Steering was by the front wheels and a separate rudder. In all, 12,778 GPAs were made, with 383 coming to the United Kingdom.*

The
legends

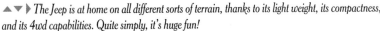

▲▼▶ *The Jeep is at home on all different sorts of terrain, thanks to its light weight, its compactness, and its 4wd capabilities. Quite simply, it's huge fun!*

The Hotchkiss Jeep: the 4x4 France loved first

▲ *Simplicity is a Jeep's forte – with just a couple of spanners you can have most of it to bits.*

The Jeep is certainly the world's pioneer four-wheel-driver. But if it generates a huge amount of passion in its country of birth, the same can also be said of one of its principal countries of adoption, by which I mean France. Now of course the Jeep was at one stage the vehicle of choice for countless armies around the world. But in France it was more than just that. In the first place, it carries with it the rich symbolism of our national liberation. It was with Jeeps that the Allies landed in Normandy in June 1944 and it was with Jeeps that the Americans – with General de Gaulle – entered Paris. Those sorts of event leave a deep mark.

Then, in the 1950s, after a false start with the over-complex Delahaye VLR, the Jeep became the obvious choice as a light vehicle for the French army, and as a result was made under licence in France by Hotchkiss, from 1955 until 1969. Called the M201, the Hotchkiss Jeep was virtually identical to the MB Jeep ('M' for 'Military' and 'B' for second version) that had served so well at the

Liberation. As you might expect, the story didn't end in 1969: right through to the end of the 1980s the Hotchkiss Jeeps remained in service, until they were gently phased out in favour of the Peugeot P4 (which is our old friend the G-Class Mercedes, only French-assembled and Peugeot-powered) and – latterly – the Auverland A3.

As a result the Jeep was the vehicle generations of French learnt to drive on, during their national service – which means that there is still a huge reserve of affection for this long-lived part of the French scenery. And since then, over the better part of 20 years, the Jeeps have been disposed of through government auctions, bringing great happiness to those lucky individuals who have been able to buy one for use as a leisure vehicle. That's why you can still find fully reconditioned as-new ex-army MBs for sale at some Jeep specialists. The example featured here is fresh out of the restoration workshop of one of the top firms in the business, Paris concern Army Pol.

▲ *The Solex carb of the Hotchkiss is one of its advantages over the original MB, as it improves both mpg and performance.*
▶ *The 2.2-litre flathead develops 60bhp at 3600rpm, and maximum torque of 103lb ft at 2000rpm.*

▲ *The gearbox is a three-speeder with a very low-ratio step-down 'box. The third lever engages 4wd via the transfer 'box.*

▶ *Simple but complete: instruments comprise an mph speedo and gauges for oil pressure, water temperature, fuel level and amps. What more do you want?*

▼ *Don't expect wood and leather. This is the army Mr Dupont…*

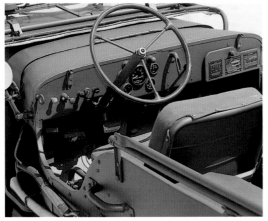

▼ *A left-over from the war, the black-out light meant you could grope your way home without being picked out by the enemy.*

▲ *The Jeep often served as a radio car, and in such cases had this aerial on its plinth. The grab-handle below aided air-lifting.*

▲ *A clever detail Ford came up with: the headlamps can be hinged back to light the engine bay, for those night-time breakdowns…*

▲▼ *On both sides and under the rear seat there are handy cubbies.*

▲▼ *The screen can be folded flat, or alternatively hinged open: how much fresh air do you want?*

▲ *The rot-proof canvas hood was all the weather protection you got; experiments with hard-tops never came to much.*

▲ *The Jeep weighs less than a ton, and its chassis was so flimsy it had to have timber reinforcements in its longerons. But off-road its light weight is a positive advantage.*

The Hummer

▲ *Park it beside a Suzuki Samurai and you get a better idea of the Hummer's extraordinary size; this is the double-cab version.*

▲ *The Hummer has all-wheel independent suspension, with variable-rate coil springs and massive wishbones.*

▲ *The air intake includes a snorkel to allow fording of water up to a depth of 4ft.*

▲ ▶ *Although it's hard to believe anything could stop it, the Hummer is additionally fitted with a hefty Warn 12,000-series winch.*

The Hummer came into the public eye in a somewhat unconventional way: it was one of the stars of the Gulf War. Because the Hummer was the brainchild of the US Army, it has played a role in the forces pretty much akin to that of a big Willys Jeep. But since then there has been a civilian version that has shown a commercial potential almost as sizeable as the beast itself, thanks to its unchallenged position as the biggest and baddest 4x4 of all time.

The Hummer has been designed to be as bombproof (almost literally) as can be, and to cope with the very worst that can be thrown at it, so anyone owning one will never more than scratch at the surface of its abilities. It has enormous wheels, formidable angles of attack and departure, Torsen automatic-locking diffs, and a 205bhp 6.5-litre turbo-diesel V8 that dishes out a whacking 440lb ft of torque at 1800rpm. As if that weren't enough, the transfer box has one of the lowest gearings you're likely to come across. Then there's the tyres, whose pressure can be adjusted from the cockpit thanks to the CTIS system, down to a pressure of around 10psi, to cope with loss of traction in difficult conditions such as sand or mud. Features such as these make one forget the Hummer's weight of 66.4cwt is that of a small lorry, and that it is a whopping 7ft 2in wide. Still crunching a few mad numbers, the 33-gallon fuel tank gives the Hummer a barely sufficient range, as it guzzles fuel at the rate of 8mpg, at a steady speed of 80mph. The price is in line, too: if you want to get behind the wheel of a Hummer, you'll have to fork out between £57,000 and £63,000 – or a little bit less in the States.

Still, the Hummer has now produced offspring. First Toyota came up with its Mega Cruiser, which is a brazen imitation of the original, albeit on a slightly more manageable scale. Then there arrived the real thing in miniature (relatively speaking) when GM, who took over the makers of the Hummer, came up with the Hummer H2. A civilian-only model, based on a regular SUV chassis, it offers a rather more practical take on the original brutalist war-wagon theme.

◀▶ *The other magic trick the Hummer has up its sleeve is the dashboard-operated inflation-deflation system for its tyres, so pressures can be changed depending on the terrain.*

▼ The engine is a huge 6474cc V8 turbo-diesel developing 205bhp at 3400rpm and maximum torque of 440lb ft at 1800rpm. It has been designed to operate in all positions and in all atmospheric conditions.

▲ The Hummer (here in Station Wagon form) faces up to its Toyota Mega Cruiser clone. The Toyota is longer, at 16ft 5¼in against 15ft 5in, but roughly an inch narrower and 5½in taller.

▼ The big innovation with the Mega is its system of four-wheel steering, which allows it turn on a sixpence – the turning circle is 36.75ft.

▼ The Hummer H2 is a General Motors product rather than a de-mobbed Army vehicle, and is built on a Chevrolet Tahoe chassis. So it's a bit of a fake, really…

▲ The H1 cockpit is huge, but the seats, pushed out to all four corners of the interior, are more than three feet apart. For all the space the H1 takes up, the driver is wedged against the door as if he were in a Willys Jeep.

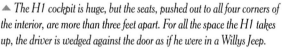

▲ No, you aren't aboard a plane! This is the Hummer H1, and amongst all the gizmos are air-con, an eight-speaker hi-fi, electric windows, and electric mirrors – the last pretty handy, given the vehicle's width.

▲ The Mega uses a Toyota lorry engine, a 4104cc four-cylinder unit developing 155bhp at 3200rpm and a maximum torque of 299lb ft at 1800rpm.

▼ The Mega interior has something in common with that of the Hummer, if only thanks to that vast central tunnel – but the finish is so much better. The auto gearbox is a four-speeder.

▲ This pick-up concept car is funky, to be sure, but it's a more mundane station wagon that has been introduced first. Power comes from a Vortec 6-litre petrol V8, developing 322bhp and a maximum torque of 362lb ft at 4000rpm.

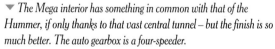

▲ These levers control the four-speed automatic, the transfer box and – operating back-to-front – the handbrake.

▲ The H2 cockpit is leagues removed from the functionalism of the H1's flight deck. In fact there's a touch of concept car about the presentation.

The Range Rover

The P38A poses with three of the first-generation range.

Before the Range Rover, the 4x4 was a rustic vehicle, with the emphasis on practicality and function. All that changed with the 1970 arrival of the Rover company's stroke of genius. The idea wasn't new: back in the 1950s Rover had built several prototype estate cars called Road-Rovers that were a halfway house between the utilitarian Land Rover and a more conventional estate. The concept was revived in the mid-1960s after market research in the US suggested that the coming thing was a more leisure-orientated breed of 4x4.

The result was a prototype built during 1967 and known as the '100in Station Wagon', on account of the length of the vehicle's wheelbase. Key features were long-travel coil-spring suspension for the front and rear rigid axles and the use of the ex-Buick 3.5-litre aluminium V8 engine. The design was one that was right, from the word 'go': even the styling of the original prototype was carried through in its essentials to the production vehicles.

Launched in June 1970, the first Range Rovers were more spartan devices than might be expected: rubber mats, vinyl seats, manual windows and an absence of power steering indicate how cautious Rover was about straying too far from the Land Rover's practicality. Off-road ability was not in doubt: the generous axle articulation and full-time 4wd actually made it a better mud-plugger than the Land Rover, yet the Boge self-levelling rear and the relatively soft springing gave it good roadholding and a comfortable ride when on tarmac.

In the shambolic days of British Leyland, supply never matched demand, and improvements were slow in coming, but power steering arrived in 1973, a factory-built four-door in 1981, an optional automatic transmission in 1982 and a five-speed manual gearbox the following year, and a VM turbo-diesel in 1986. All along the way, the interior became progressively more luxurious, as the Range Rover inched its way further up-market. The final versions of the first-series Range Rover could be obtained with anti-roll bars front and rear (from late 1990), while for 1993 air suspension was introduced on a new longer-wheelbase LSE model and on the Vogue SE.

It was only in 1994 that the original was replaced by the all-new second-series Range Rover. Coded P38A, this had a relatively short life, giving way in 2002 to the current impressive model.

▲ Badged 'Velar', a made-up name, this is the sixth prototype built, and dates from 1969. The Range Rover's secret was its long-travel coil-spring suspension, mated with the V8 engine and permanent four-wheel drive.

◀ The Range Rover was largely unchanged for many years, because BL didn't have the money to invest in Solihull. This 1975 model has the vinyl-covered rear pillars introduced in 1973, and a non-standard fuel-filler flap.

▲▼ In mid-1984 a new dashboard was introduced, sharing its instrument cluster with the Austin Maestro; automatic transmission had been available since 1982.

▼ It was a Range Rover that won the first Paris–Dakar in 1979, courtesy Frenchmen Genestier, Terbault and Lemordant. The car was subsequently a regular contender in other off-road events.

▲ The five-door version, on the same wheelbase as the two-door, only arrived in 1981 – although a prototype had been built as early as 1972. More luxurious trim was introduced at around the same time.

▲ The Range Rover was available with a VM turbo-diesel from 1986 – initially a 2398cc unit developing 112bhp at 4200rpm. From late 1986 there was a new grille, with horizontal slats, and concealed bonnet hinges. The 3947cc engine arrived for 1990, delivering 185bhp at 4750rpm.

▲ The LSE, launched in 1992, had an 8in longer wheelbase (allowing bigger rear doors) and air suspension; power came from an enlarged 4278cc V8 with an output of 200bhp at 4850rpm.

▲ The second-generation Range Rover was launched at the 1994 British motor show. It kept the same wheelbase as the LSE, and air suspension was standard, still in conjunction with rigid axles front and rear. Petrol versions used 3.9-litre and 4.6-litre V8s.

▲ The BMW turbo-diesel engine was chosen before the German company bought Rover Group, and was the catalyst for the acquisition; output is 136bhp at 4400rpm. Despite the move up-market, the Range Rover sacrificed none of its off-road ability.

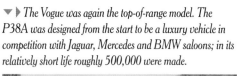

▼ ▶ The Vogue was again the top-of-range model. The P38A was designed from the start to be a luxury vehicle in competition with Jaguar, Mercedes and BMW saloons; in its relatively short life roughly 500,000 were made.

▼ Studies for a third generation began in 1998, with BMW firmly in the driving seat. The L322 was intended to be bigger and better than its predecessor in all areas.

▼ The new Range Rover has monocoque construction and all-independent suspension by front struts and rear twin wishbones. Steering, engine and gearbox are all ex-BMW, although Ford's takeover means this will change in the future.

▲ ▼ As before, the Range Rover is built in the former Rover works in Solihull. The photo shows a line of Range Rover MkIs going down the lines; things have changed plenty since those days.

▼ ▼ The interior of the new Range Rover has won much praise for its imaginative design, with pale wood trim on top-of-range models. We're a long way from the spartan original of 1970…

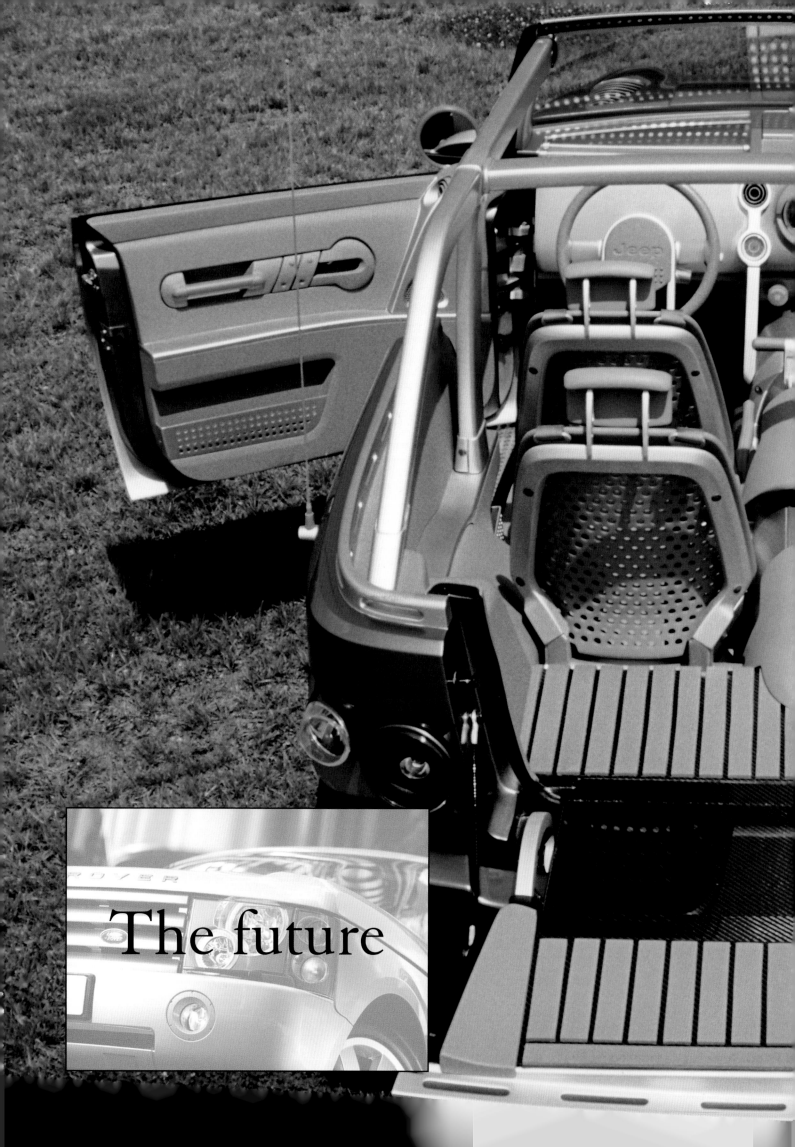

The future

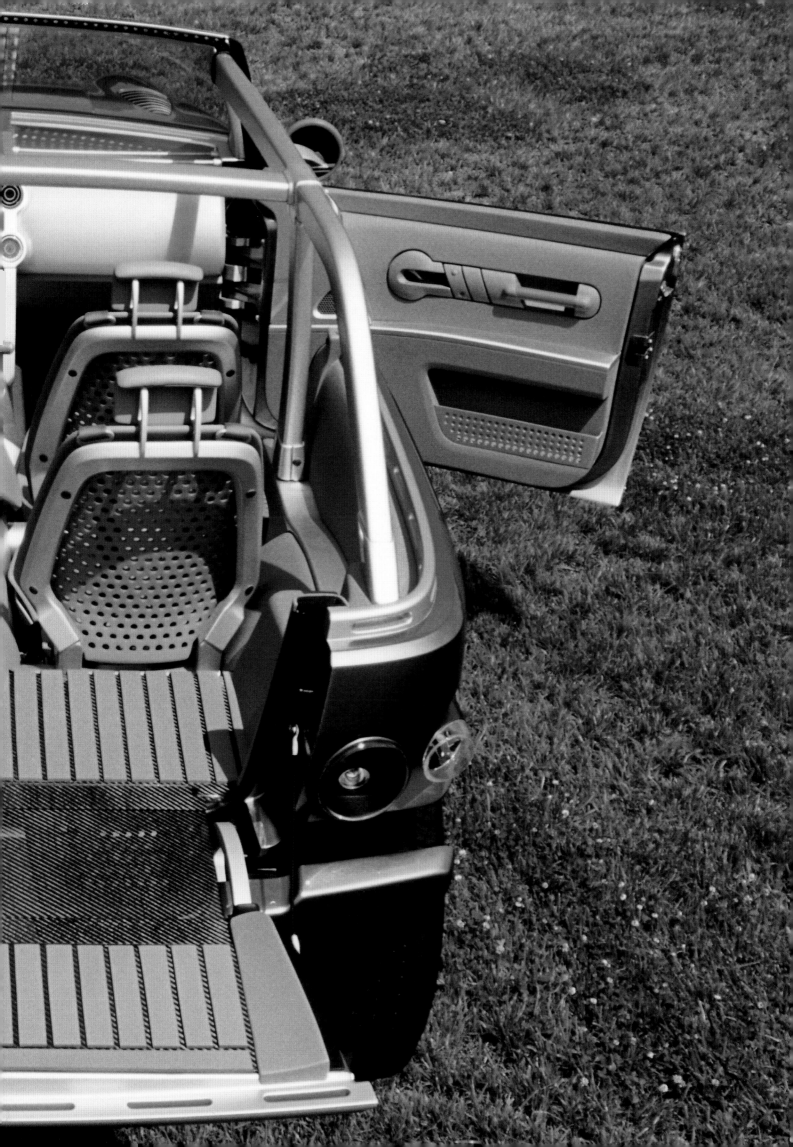

▲ *The Ford F350 Tonka is just the kind of prototype that could end up on a dealership floor. It is stupendously big: 20ft long, nearly 8ft wide, and 7ft high. The wheels are 22-inchers, and the 350bhp 6-litre V8 wallops out 599lb ft of torque at 2000rpm.*

▼ *After the tank-like exterior the interior, with its clap-hands doors, seems almost refined. Only the sprung driver's seat betrays a certain truck flavour…*

The States: still taking the crazy pills…

In some ways the Americans are just big kids – and if you want proof, take a look at their cars. Mad, over-the-top: somehow nothing seems to shock them, or hold them back. And the car manufacturers join in, with the advantage that the 4x4 of the Average Joe is already a far more eccentric device than anything you'd see on the streets anywhere else in the world.

Not convinced? Well, take the Hummer H2. This saw the light of day as the ever-so-slightly-nuts 'Baby Hummer' concept, and yet it wasn't long before you could tool down to your local car-dealer mall and buy one off the showroom floor.

Sure, some of these concepts will never make it to production, but you can never be certain, given how carefully the feedback from displaying these cars at the big auto shows (Detroit, Chicago, Los Angeles or New York) is studied. If there's been a generally positive reaction from the press and the public, that can tip the balance, and a futurist dream car can become a scarcely less extravagant production model.

All the major marques bring their skill and originality to bear when it comes to these show cars – and particularly so when we're talking pick-ups, as these are so much in fashion. In fact things have reached such a pitch that the Japanese have now joined in, and are turning out concept cars not much less wild than those of the US firms. It's just a shame that at present there doesn't seem to be much of a chance that the bug will spread to sober-sided old Europe…

▶ *The Dodge M80 is aimed above all at lovers of out-doors sports such as surfing, skiing and mountain-biking. Its light weight is a key feature, as is the lively 210bhp V6 which seems to go with the zingy yellow paintwork.*

▼ *The Willys II could hint at the next Jeep Wrangler. With its 21in wheels, 12in ground clearance, non-existent overhangs and high-low transfer box, it has all the right ingredients for getting down and dirty.*

▲ ▲ *The Jeep Compass is based on the Cherokee, and uses its 210bhp 3.7-litre V6. It stands out on account of its small size (it's less than 14ft long) and its low centre of gravity. The interior, right down to the sporty seat harnesses, picks up on the khaki colour of the exterior.*

◀ *The modern looks of the Willys II and the performance of its 1.6-litre 160bhp turbocharged engine suggest a degree of versatility. It is so well executed that a production version is surely not beyond hope.*

◀ *The Jeep Commander concept trailed the basic styling direction of the new Grand Cherokee. Powered by fuel-cells, it showcases Daimler-Chrysler advanced technology. The body is entirely in plastic – another portent for the future?*

▼ *Ford has gone to the other extreme from the Tonka with its EX. This buggy with its outrageous 360bhp V6 turbo is intended for pure let-your-hair-down pleasure.*

▼ *The Ford EX has just two seats, set in a stripped-down sports-flavoured cockpit. The tubular chassis incorporates a hefty roll-cage, and the seats can slide up and down on rails.*

▲ *The Chevrolet SSR is certainly an aesthetic success, mixing the curved lines of the classic American pick-up with a stripped-bare modernism. The roof retracts, roadster-style. Given the effort that's gone into the SSR, wouldn't it be nice if it made it to production, maybe with a 6.0-litre V8 under the bonnet? One can but dream…*

▶ *The detailing on the SSR is gorgeous. Just look at how the rear wing sweeps over that huge 20in wheel…*

▼ *This enormous full-size truck, the GMC Terra 4, uses a 6.6-litre turbo-diesel engine from GM affiliate Isuzu, linked to a five-speed automatic. It is built on one of GMC's existing platforms.*

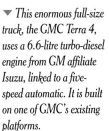

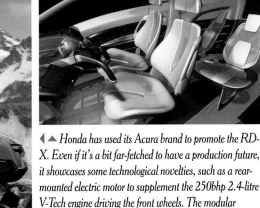

◀▲ *Honda has used its Acura brand to promote the RD-X. Even if it's a bit far-fetched to have a production future, it showcases some technological novelties, such as a rear-mounted electric motor to supplement the 250bhp 2.4-litre V-Tech engine driving the front wheels. The modular interior, with its movable seats, pedals and dashboard, testifies to its leisure role, as does the three-piece tailgate. Electronics include a head-up instrument display and a reversing camera.*

▼▼ *The Terra 4 dashboard and interior are cleanly designed; the pick-up rear is wonderfully versatile, with cantilevered side panels and a sliding deck cover.*

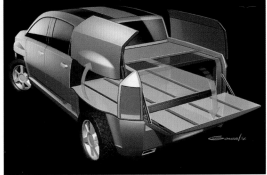

▶ *The Montero Evolution coupé was no mere show car: it developed into the Pajero Evolution that scored a 1–2 for Mitsubishi in the 2004 Dakar.*

▲ *Here it is again, only in a more effective matt grey. With a 4.7-litre V8 from the gloriously tasteless Proudia luxo-barge, plus a sequential six-speed gearbox, this sexed-up 2+2 looked as if it should sure kick ass…*

▼ *The bucket seats with integral harness show that the guys at Mitsubishi mean business.*

▼ *A pull-out drawer provides tidy stowage for vital equipment, from a multi-tool to a sat-nav, not forgetting a first-aid kit and a hip-flask….and four helmets, of course.*

Asia: still as inventive as ever

The Japanese have always had a weakness for motor shows. For years we've had the spectacle of their designers running amok at Tokyo, coming up with concept after concept, and with each one being nuttier than the one before – whether a microcar, a minibus, a sports coupé…or a 4x4 any which way you want it. As far as the last category is concerned, three trends have emerged from the ponderings of these switched-on wild men of design: big American-flavoured 4x4s, micro-4x4s that are a combination of town-car and MPV, and finally competition 4x4s that seem to be a Mad Max take on what you might see on the 2027 Paris–Dakar.

Whichever way you slice it, there's nothing too serious bubbling away, and nobody's inclined to complain. With these show cars the Japanese – and also the Koreans – trot out pretty extreme stuff, but as much as anything as a way of proving their ingeniousness and skill and adding a bit of dynamism to their marque image. They also seem to be looking further ahead than those in the US or Europe: they're seeking out new trends, new ways forward. In this they are closer to the spirit that motivated the great concept cars of the past – as opposed to what happens so often these days, when a concept car is frequently little more than a pre-production version of something that will be in the showroom in a year or two.

Here then is a selection of vehicles that are probably less likely to see the light of day than their US equivalents but which all the same give some pointers to future trends – perhaps, indeed, some good way into the future.

▶ *The Toyota RSC looks like Toyota's take on the same theme, and again looks ready for a future 'Dakar'. Helping it along, it's based on a World Rally Championship Toyota.*

◀ *Japan's Number One has kept quiet about the power unit, and about its intentions for the car. Could Toyota be thinking about locking horns with rival Mitsubishi, in the Paris–Dakar?*

▼ *The interior is pure competition in style, with carbon-fibre bucket seats, harnesses, and a sequential gearbox.*

▲ *The Mitsubishi SUP is supposedly named after the phrase 'What's up?'. Believe that if you will, but you have to ask what the designers did have in mind…*

▲◀ *The SUP is stuffed with clever gadgetry. The doors hold removable cases to take fishing or camping equipment or a tool set, and there's even an integral shower – so handy after a day on the beach…*

▲ *Nissan's Crossbow is a modernist sculptural interpretation of the Hummer look, motorised by a 300bhp 4.5-litre V8. The clap-hands doors open to reveal a huge passenger compartment with four separate seats.*

▼ *The cockpit has an aircraft feel about it – just clock that transmission shifter! – and features a huge sat-nav screen.*

▲ *The Isuzu GBX could develop into a replacement for the Trooper; certainly these functionalist-brutalist lines are taste of the moment. At least the GBX is a manageable size, at less than 15ft long.*

▼ *Inside there are three rows of seats and a suitably futurist dashboard with sat-nav, computer and so on.*

▲ *According to Nissan's man in charge of 4x4s the Crossbow could form the basis of the next-generation Patrol. Please form an orderly queue…*

▼ *Finally, here's a concept car that has made it to production. Honda's Model X, suicide rear doors and all, is made in Ohio for the US market, as the Element; power comes from a 2354cc 'four' delivering 160bhp, and 2wd and 4wd versions are available.*

▲ *Daewoo's Vada has a good ground clearance, with its 18in wheels, and with its pneumatic self-levelling independent suspension promises good off-road performance; power comes from a 140bhp 2-litre twin-cam.*

▶ *Roomy (it's a six-seater) and with easy access, thanks to its pillarless design and suicide rear doors, the Mercedes GST (Grand Sport Tourer) has an interior like a museum of modern art.*

▼ *Nearly 17ft long, slightly jacked up on its suspension, and with elaborate full-time 4wd, the GST will see production as the R-Class – less the fancy rear-hinged back doors.*

▼ *The GST has Air-Matic suspension, based on that of the S-Class, and a 360bhp AMG-tuned 5.5-litre V8. Production versions will use various V6s and V8s.*

▼ *The Saab 9-3X hides a full-time 4wd set-up under its sporting-estate bodywork. But will this exciting concept lead anywhere for the now GM-owned Swedish firm?*

▼ *The engine of the 9-3X is a new direct-injection 2.8-litre turbo V6 pushing out 280bhp and a healthy 295lb ft of torque at 1700rpm – making the Saab good for a claimed 0–60mph time of 6.2 seconds, with decent economy.*

Europe: brewing up nicely…

In this scrabble for new markets, Europe didn't for some while seem to be much turned on by the 4x4 thing. There was a sort of no-man's land as far as 4wd concept cars were concerned, this at a time when the creative juices were most definitely flowing in other sectors, and giving birth to such innovatory machines as the Scénic and the Smart. But in the space of a few years the old continent seems to have caught up – the others had better watch out!

Leading the way has been Germany, which has piled full-bore into the luxury end of 4x4 concept-car dreamland. All the signs are that this effervescence is going to trickle downwards, too, giving birth to more accessible SUVs in the RAV4 and Freelander mould. And what about reinventing those old favourites? How about Land-Rover going back to its roots and coming up with a new stripped-to-the-bone Defender? Then there's Mercedes: a modern take on the G-Class could go down a storm…

In all this, though, there's been one country that has held back, and that's France. We saw a very promising concept car from Renault, in the shape of the Koleos, yet it was soon swirling down the plughole in the wake of the Renault-Nissan marriage, as Nissan was seen as the combine's 4x4 specialist. As for PSA, with the exception of the Citroën C-Crosser, with its airy-fairy off-roadability, the group really doesn't seem interested. That's a real shame, given the past history of the two marques, Citroën with those ground-breaking *croisières* and Peugeot with its traditional presence in Africa. *C'est la vie…*

◀ *The 9-3X interior keeps a Saab flavour. Equipment is lavish, and includes an on-board computer to look after a rear-view camera, sat-nav, telephone, and a top-range hi-fi.*

▼ *The least you can say is that the Magellan is seen by VW as a vehicle for the Great Outdoors!*

◀ *It might carry a VW badge, but the Magellan is more likely to emerge as an SUV Audi built on the Cayenne/Touareg platform. Expect the 313bhp V10 Tdi, a 275bhp W8 and a fire-breathing 420bhp W12.*

◀ *Behind the wheel of the Magellan you could be in the cockpit of an aircraft – quite some change from VW's usual drab interiors.*

▶ *The Audi Steppenwolf is a bit like a 4x4 version of the Audi TT. Aesthetically resolved and well-executed, it would be nice if something came of the project.*

▼ *The Steppenwolf has four-level air suspension and Audi's quattro 4wd transmission. The engine is a relatively sober 225bhp V6...*

◀ *The VW's rear suicide doors are cleverly disguised; they open to reveal a full four-seat interior, beautifully presented.*
▼ *The VW AAC is a four-door pick-up concept based on the Touareg. What price the production of a more realistic version for the US market?*

▼ *The Project SVX Land Rover hints at some design directions a new Defender might take – one day, perhaps...*

▶ *The Renault Koleos had French enthusiasts hoping it would lead to the marque entering the 4x4 market. But it now seems as if the project won't lead to anything concrete.*
▼ *The Citroën C-Crosser has the original feature of a driving position that can be switched from left to right: how nice of the French to think of the British...*

▼ *The C-Crosser is something of a surprise, coming from Citroën. A leisure vehicle mixing modular MPV and off-roader, with a fun shape and adjustable-height hydractive suspension: sounds too good to stay on the shelf!*

GLOSSARY

ABS: Anti-lock brakes. Electronic regulation of brake application to avoid wheels locking under severe braking. Now a legal requirement on all new cars.

Acceleration Slip Regulation: Part of Porsche's PTM system (Porsche Traction Management) on the Cayenne. When traction is lost, ASR reduces engine output until traction is restored.

Air suspension: Increasingly common on top-range 4x4s, as it allows adjustment of levels, either manually or automatically. Based around pneumatic cylinders that replace the springs.

All Mode: Nissan 4x4 system used on X-Trail. When car is in Auto mode, only front wheels are driven. Sensors link engine ECU and electronic throttle control with 4wd and ABS controller: wheel slippage sends signals to electro-magnetic centre clutch to distribute torque to rear axle as appropriate.

Anti-roll bar: useful for countering roll, especially on a high-built 4x4. On some vehicles the anti-roll bars can be disconnected for off-road use, allowing greater axle articulation.

Approach angle: Maximum angle of slope a vehicle can attack without fouling its front bumper or running aground.

Axle: strictly speaking the term should only be used for a rigid beam linking right-hand and left-hand wheels – in other words when the wheels in question are not independently sprung. Traditional 4x4s such as Land-Rovers retain rigid axles front and rear, resulting in better off-road ability.

Clutch: something to be avoided as much as possible when off-roading. If you de-clutch when the vehicle is in a critical position, such as going down a slope, engine braking will be lost and with it any control over the vehicle's momentum. Best engage low-ratio and use low gears, even at the risk of stalling.

Command-Trac: Jeep selectable 4wd system, used on Wrangler.

Departure angle: maximum angle at which a vehicle can climb without fouling its rear end.

Diesel: Ideal engine for an off-roader, because it has excellent torque, and delivers its maximum pulling power low down the rev range. Greater flywheel inertia helps engine braking, too.

Differential lock: Normally a differential allows the two wheels on the same axle to turn at different speeds. But in certain off-road situations (such as when one wheel is off the ground or on a slippery surface), it can help to be able to lock the diff so that full power is transmitted to the wheel that has been left to do all the work. These days a dashboard switch generally operates the diff lock(s), but on something such as an early Mercedes G-Class there are two separate knobs on the transmission tunnel.

Differential, central: In normal conditions of grip (ie on tarmac), in a curve the front and rear wheels of a car don't cover the same distance. To compensate for this 'over-run', permanent 4wd vehicles have a central differential which distributes engine power between front and rear axles and takes the stress off the propshaft. Off-road, any lack of adhesion can be countered by locking this central differential.

Differential, limited-slip: Differential that starts to lock up automatically, as soon as the difference in speed between the two wheels exceeds a certain point – ie one wheel starts to lose adhesion. As a result the power passes to the wheel where adhesion is greater. In off-road use an LSD is less effective than a manual diff lock (see above).

Downhill Assist Control: Toyota's take on Hill Descent Control, standard on automatic Land Cruisers. Operates brakes automatically at speeds below 15mph, with no pressure on brake or accelerator pedals needed.

EBD (Electronic Brake Distribution): Electronic system that distributes braking effort to give maximum stability under braking.

ESP (Electronic Stability Programme): electronic control of engine power delivery and brakes, linked through ABS system. Increasingly common on 4x4s, under various names (eg Vehicle Stability Control, or VSC, in case of Toyota).

Hill Descent Control: Land Rover system first seen on Freelander. Limits speed and avoids wheel lock-up; operates through ABS circuits.

Hill-start Assist Control: Electronic system avoiding wheelspin or slipping backwards when hill-starting with an automatic. Pioneered by Toyota on its 2004 Land Cruiser automatics. Manual-transmission Porsche Cayennes have an analogous device called the Porsche Drive-off Assistant.

Hubs, freewheel: Allow the front wheels to freewheel, by disconnecting drive from the front differential to the hub. Originally had to be engaged by hand, but now generally actuated by electrics.

Quadra-Drive: Jeep permanent 4wd system used principally on V8 versions of Grand Cherokee. Development of Quadra-Trac (see below), using progressive torque-sensing ('Vari-Lok') front and rear differentials.

Quadra-Trac II: Jeep permanent 4wd system used on Grand Cherokee. Features electronic distribution of engine power between front and rear wheels.

Rallye-raid: A French institution, so we'll keep it in the French. A test of competitive driving and navigation, as often as not in North Africa or another part of the African continent. The clasic example is the Paris–Dakar.

Ramp break-over angle: A measure of a vehicle's ability to drive over a sharp ridge or ramp without touching its underside. A short-wheelbase design with high ground clearance and large tyres has the best ramp breakover angle.

Road book: The route book for a rally, giving detailed directions, generally diagramatically (called 'tulips' by the Brits…).

Sand ladders: The only way of getting out of soft sand. Also useful in some muddy conditions. Go for those made of aluminium rather than plastic. Don't forget to dig them out afterwards, as they often sink out of sight!

Selec-Trac: Jeep permanent 4wd system used on some Cherokees.

SS4-I: 'Intelligent' selectable 4wd system with viscous coupling, used on Mitsubishi Shogun Pinin GDI.

Sumpguard: Sometimes called a skidplate, and a most handy fixing. In steel, aluminium or reinforced plastic, it protects the sump and sometimes the whole of the front-end mechanicals. Helpful, too, for sliding over crests in sand-dunes and flattening vegetation in the middle of a rutted track.

Suspension, independent: Old-hat on road cars, but a relatively recent innovation on off-roaders, for the simple reason that rigid axles give a constant ground clearance and thus better off-road ability. But with the requirement for 4x4s to have acceptable ride, roadholding and handling on tarmac, the use of independent suspension at the front, and

generally also now at the rear, has become commonplace. A satisfactory halfway house is to have an independent front but a well-located coil-sprung rigid rear axle.

Suspension: You'll find coil springs, leaf springs and torsion bars are all used on 4x4s. Old-fashioned leaf springs are becoming less common, but are still to be found, especially on the back end of pick-ups; as for torsion bars the main user of these was Mitsubishi, on its first and second series of Shogun.

Terrain Response System: Land Rover dial-adjustable control of vehicle systems (including ride height), dependent on terrain symbol selected; introduced on Discovery 3.

Torsen differential: Literally 'Torque Sensing', this is an evolution of the traditional limited-slip differential, and is particularly common as a central diff, as it can adjust the torque split between front and rear axles in response to differing levels of adhesion.

Traction Control: Many different systems exist, but the basic principle is that sensors at each wheel measure traction and brake the wheel in question as appropriate.

Transfer box: Auxiliary gearbox that effects the transfer between four-wheel drive and two-wheel drive. Generally incorporates reduction gearing (non synchronised) to allow a lowering of all gear ratios by roughly half, for off-road use: the result is more torque, better flexibility, and improved engine braking.

Tripmaster: electric mileometer that records distances with more precision than an ordinary speedo trip. Records partial and overall mileages. An indispensible accompaniment to your road book…

Turbocharger: an exhaust-driven turbine that delivers air under pressure to the combustion chambers. Most diesels in 4x4s have a turbo these days, and a good turbo-diesel has a power output not far off that of a normally-aspirated petrol engine of the same capacity, while retaining the diesel's virtues of low fuel consumption and excellent low-range torque. Make sure you use a good oil: turbocharger turbines turn at over 200,000rpm.

Tyre pressures: In off-road use you can reduce pressure to roughly 15psi to have better traction in mud and sand. You'll be amazed at the difference it will make. But watch out for two things. First, don't over-deflate, or you'll risk twisting the tyre off its seating or even losing it off the wheel. Secondly, once you're on terra firma, don't forget to pump the tyres up again, or else you'll have a blow-out.

Tyres: Mixed-use all-terrain tyres are normal wear on 4x4s used both on tarmac and off-road, but there are plenty of special rugged-tread 'mud-terrain' tyres available for trialling. For sand use, specialists can supply suitable tyres as well.

Viscous coupling: Used either as a differential or as a means of automatically actuating the locking of a diff. The coupling relies on the

changing viscosity (stickiness, in plain English) of the special silicone oil in which it runs. It is composed of a series of discs that normally rotate freely in the coupling. The moment that the two driveshafts it controls (say from the front and the rear wheels, in the case of a central diff) begin to rotate at different speeds, heat is generated, causing the oil to thin and the discs to lock up to a greater or lesser degree, as the cushioning provided by the oil's stickiness disappears.

Weight transfer: A basic physical characteristic of a motor car, the weight shifting towards the front or the rear, depending on whether one brakes or accelerates. On a 4x4 the phenomenon is more acute, owing to the high centre of gravity and the more generous suspension travel the vehicles possess. Off-road, weight transfer is exploited to get the front to dig in, by applying the brakes, with a little bit of lock, as you enter a curve. The rear will step sideways, and you can play with 'controlled drifts'. Just make sure you know what you're doing…

Wheelbase: a long wheelbase will mean more comfort and better roadholding, but a short wheelbase will make the vehicle more agile and easier to handle. Your call…

Winch: The fifth driven wheel on a 4x4! Whether fixed or detachable, it will get you out of the most difficult situations, particularly if you're on your own. If you're bogged down, or stuck in the sand, it's usually possible to extricate yourself, with a bit of skill, from whatever mess you've landed yourself in.

INDEX

The pages in **bold** refer to sections specifically devoted to the subject in question